HUMMER

HUMMER

HOW A LITTLE TRUCK COMPANY HIT THE BIG TIME, THANKS TO SADDAM, SCHWARZENEGGER, AND GM

MARTY PADGETT

MOTORBOOKS
INTERNATIONAL

First published in 2004 by Motorbooks International, an imprint of
MBI Publishing Company, Galtier Plaza, Suite 200, 380 Jackson Street, St. Paul, MN
55101-3885 USA

© Marty Padgett, 2004

All rights reserved. With the exception of quoting brief passages for the purposes of review, no part of this publication may be reproduced without prior written permission from the Publisher.

The information in this book is true and complete to the best of our knowledge.
All recommendations are made without any guarantee on the part of the author or Publisher, who also disclaim any liability incurred in connection with the use of this data or specific details.

This publication has not been prepared, approved, or licensed by General Motors. We recognize, further, that some words, model names, and designations mentioned herein are the property of the trademark holder. We use them for identification purposes only. This is not an official publication.

Motorbooks International titles are also available at discounts in bulk quantity for industrial or sales-promotional use. For details write to Special Sales Manager at Motorbooks International Wholesalers & Distributors, Galtier Plaza, Suite 200,
380 Jackson Street, St. Paul, MN 55101-3885 USA.

ISBN 0-7603-1863-8

Edited by Peter Schletty
Cover design by Mandy Iverson
Layout by Tom Heffron

Printed in the USA

Contents

Dedication 6

Acknowledgments 7

Introduction 9

Chapter 1   **Birth of a Nation—of SUVs**   17

Chapter 2   **A HUMMER Is Born**   43

Chapter 3   **The Road to Baghdad—and Beyond**   59

Chapter 4   **The Terminator and the Hummer**   85

Chapter 5   **War and Peace**   99

Chapter 6   **GM Wants In**   119

Chapter 7   **H2: Stinger Missiles and Soccer Moms**   153

Chapter 8   **Anti-SUV Hysteria, or Arianna Takes On the H2**   179

Chapter 9   **Back to Baghdad**   201

Chapter 10 **As Good As It Gets**   227

Resources   247

Photo Credits   252

Index   253

Dedication

To my sister, for teaching me to read; my parents, for encouraging me to write; and most of all to Jack, for telling me when to put the book down.

Acknowledgments

Many people were instrumental in getting me to write a book, getting this one done and guiding me through the process. I've grouped them here in ways that make sense to me:

People who know a lot more than I do, and let me share the credit: Mike Davis, Paul Eisenstein, David Kiley, Joe Szczesny

People who made me want to write more: Jill Amadio, David Claypool, Shari Grimes, John Pearley Huffman, William Jeanes, Virginia Pickett, Bob Weil, Carol Williams.

People who made it pay: James Fitzgerald, Peter Schletty.

And for their participation, assistance and expertise:

AM General: Craig Mac Nab, Steve Spengler, Bill Thompson and all the instructors at the HUMMER Driving Academy

HUMMER and General Motors: Mike DiGiovanni, Ken Lindensmith, Marc Hernandez, Keith Donovan, Wendy Orthman, Heather Hall, Joe Jacuzzi, Jeff Holland, Bob Lutz, Steve Harris and Tom Kowaleski. Also, Dr. Kevin Borg, Timothy Malefyt and Keith Bradsher

Introduction

"This is your last chance!"

Sounds like an action-movie come-on? It's not dialogue, unless you're inside my head taking down lines. When it comes to the history of HUMMER, you have an immediate choice to make—either you believe it's one of the coolest, most ingenious pieces of Americana ever devised and you stick with me for the next couple hundred pages, or you drop this book, back away from the stacks and head for the latté counter instead or run to catch your flight before they make the last cattle call for boarding.

You might have guessed that this book is about HUMMER—clever you, finding it disguised on the cover. But this isn't the rags-to-riches story of the military contractor, not the whiz-kid tale of the GM brand, and surely not the parable of how today's celebrities bought HUMMERs and promptly sank into a life of drink and drugs. Well, actually, it is about all those things, but it's also about something even larger. And you thought there was nothing larger, didn't you?

No, this book is about something larger than life, something more esoteric than action-hero stunts behind the wheel of the military's best-ever war wagon. It's about the vehicle that you'd see if you asked a ten-year-old to draw an Army vehicle. It's about the wheeled equivalent to a flag or the Statue of Liberty. It's an iconography of the four-wheeler that's taken over the world, literally and figuratively, more quickly than any truck in history and did it all in less time than it took Al "Global Warming" Gore to win a presidential race. (What, he still hasn't?)

It's about HUMMER, the phenomenon—the story of how AM General invented the Humvee and made it indispensable to the modern military, how GM used its marketing prowess and a coming internal revolution to hit a home run off AM General's pitch. And it's a study of how the SUV crisis of conscience empowered a generation of self-righteous zealots who knighted the HUMMER H2 as king of the gas guzzlers, and, depending on how much you believe, one of the seminal causes of the Sept. 11 attacks on America.

HUMMER wouldn't have attracted all this attention, both good and bad, unless it were something extraordinary. By any measure it's the most unbelievable, the most audacious, the most off-road-capable SUV on the planet. And in a day when most SUVs claim their heritage includes both off-roading expertise and on-road comfort, only the HUMMER can claim it goes from the driving range to the missile range with the flick of a locking differential switch.

Today, surveys find that HUMMER is the number-one aspirational vehicle for people under 18 years old. But how did we get here from the lowly working-class origins of the SUV? How did HUMMER become such a fundamental and controversial icon of American might within such a short span of time? Was it coincidence or cunning that made the HUMMER such an audaciously well-timed hit—or both?

To understand any of these questions, you have to dig deep into the history of American car culture, military pride and the evolution of the SUV. The HUMMER brand blends each of these strands into a uniquely twisted piece of DNA that gives it credentials that nearly no other SUV can claim.

The story of HUMMER is a chaotic one. What you know today as the H1 and H2 owes a lot to gradually changing American tastes as much as it owes to three epoch-making forces of late twentieth century American popular culture: Saddam Hussein, Arnold Schwarzenegger, and General Motors, each one a benefactor in making the HUMMER the hottest hip-hop accessory since gold teeth.

The HUMMER brand has its roots in the primordial ooze of the turn-of-the-century U.S. auto industry, when companies that eventually became American Motors Corp. (AMC) absorbed the off-road companies selling utilitarian farm vehicles to the heartland in the 1930s and 1940s. But by the time the challenge to create the original High Mobility Multi-Purpose Wheeled Vehicle (HMMWV) had begun, AMC had entered a death spiral. Desperately trying to eke any profit out of its divisions as it began augering in during the early 1970s, AMC put its AM General division up for sale after the military issued its challenge to its contractors for a new type of four-wheel military appliance—what would become the original Humvee. AM General eventually won the competition through American-style ingenuity, but the victory wouldn't mean a stable business—in fact it meant the opposite, as AM General lurched into dark financial waters several times during the Humvee's infancy and adolescence.

The first missions fought by the Humvee forged its ironclad reputation for durability and go-anywhere gumption. It had been in military fleets for nearly 12 years when it finally was battle-tested in Panama, then in the first Persian Gulf war against Saddam Hussein's army. Iraq had invaded Kuwait—and thanks to CNN, the Humvee invaded the American conscience. With a victory behind it and a decade-long infatuation with SUVs about to begin, the time was ripe for AM General to take the "Hummer" to prime time.

It might not have happened save for a big cheerleader in the form of Arnold Schwarzenegger. The future governor of California saw the Humvee in action during the war and, by all accounts, couldn't live without one. After a few phone calls and trips to AM General's headquarters in northern Indiana, he convinced AM General to prep the Humvee for sale to the general public, with himself as the first customer. (If only Schwarzenegger were born in Orange County instead of Austria, both his and its red-white-and-blue credentials would be unassailably American.) And within a year, AM General had begun selling copies of the Hummer for $50,000 apiece and more to celebs like Tom Clancy, Shaquille O'Neal, and any civilian with the scratch to own a cousin to a piece of military history. Never mind the fact that it weighed more than two tons and could barely keep highway speeds with its diesel engine—the Hummer was hot.

Over the course of the last 15 years, Schwarzenegger has become a major film star, hugely successful entrepreneur and philanthropist, and now Governor of California. But all along, he's been an unofficial and official ambassador for the HUMMER brand, and a critical figure in fusing the vehicles' military and celebrity personalities together. Without him—and without Hussein's army—there would be no strong link between the soldiers plying Humvees in Iraq and attorneys driving HUMMERs home in San Diego.

The two took the HUMMER name to new heights. While both Hussein and Schwarzenegger ruled California-sized domains with ungovernable, fractious populations—Sunnis and Shi'ites, Berkeley leftists and Irvine conservatives—they also ruled the imagery of HUMMER, one giving it internationally recognizable military context, the other giving it the macho, testosterone-driven means to segue into a civilian action hero role.

War changed America's Humvee awareness. And because of it, AM General saw more potential than it could afford to fulfill. So it enlisted one final ally in its quest to make the HUMMER more than just a household name. With the decade of SUV mania still growing in 2000, General Motors arranged a coup of its own, inking a deal that would let it use the HUMMER name for a new range of smaller SUVs that GM could sell at a massive per-vehicle profit in its own dealerships, paying AM General a licensing fee on each one. And in one of the more oddly synchronized coincidences in history, when the civilian HUMMER H2 was ready for market in 2002, a Bush was back in the White House, Arnold was back on the silver screen, and Saddam Hussein was once again at the top of the world's political agenda.

Nailing down the HUMMER's appeal is an altogether fuzzier prospect, but as you read along you'll see it's a composite of many little trends and major societal changes in American life.

A major theme, of course, is the military connection. HUMMER was birthed by the Pentagon and AM General, and like aviator jackets, Jeeps, and GPS navigation before it, it became widely accepted as part of the cultural *lingua franca*. It's a suburban appliance, too, with the introduction of the $50,000 H2—but still, it's most strongly seen as a military weapon with extreme capabilities and uses. The SUV silhouette engenders strength and bravado, while its very name conjures images of defense and aggression. It's militaristic to its very core and in coincidental, subtle ways: one of AM General's key suppliers is in Defiance, Ohio; the president of the company is named Armour.

HUMMERs are also pure Americana, conceived by the military, birthed by the heartland, now nutured by the country's biggest automaker. In a day when German cars are seen as the technological superiors and Japanese cars, the epitome of functionality and reliability, the HUMMER is a true American hero, unabashedly patriotic and singularly desirable because it's a product of the good old U.S. of A. Too, it's the most wanted vehicle inside the Beltway and outside Washington. Kids who can't pick out their home state on a map can spot an H2 from blocks away. It's the rare happening that's as hip for Generation Y as it is for the Baby Boomers.

And as sport-utility vehicles, HUMMERs are a part of the most rapid reconfiguration of the U.S. auto fleet in generations. In the past decade and a half, the SUV has simply overtaken the American auto market, zooming from less than 10 percent of total sales to more than 20 percent. Lumped in with their truck cousins, they account for more than half of the vehicles sold in America today. Sport-utility vehicles are a potent symbol of our decade, as much of their time as the Model T was of the early twentieth century.

And it's also a heavy dose of déja vu. Whether it was 13 years or 13 months ago, your nightly news carried nonstop coverage of war with Iraq. Front and center in nearly every video frame? Not the tactical weapons being fired off camera, or the aircraft flying night missions to pound Baghdad into submission. The most riveting and omnipresent image from the firefight was, more often than not, the vehicle bred specifically for military use—the Humvee.

And then, in the first commercial break, comes the payoff—for GM, for AM General, and for American marketing brilliance, all in an epic (some would say crass) thunderclap of commerce booming straight into history. The ad: one for General Motors' HUMMER H2, a simple image of the gargantuan SUV sunning itself in some non-com desert, untethered to a caravan of supply-chain logistics and unfettered by the odd sniper fire. Uncompromised, unburdened by context, and undeniably American.

Introduction

It's "Like nothing else."

In the interests of disclosure, I'm an automotive writer and have been for 15 years. If you watch *20/20* or read hypersensitive, sky-is-falling books by politically agitated writers (agitated by different politics than mine, that is) and believe them, you'll probably disregard me as polluted by the sometimes incestuous nature of the car industry, which provides me test vehicles to drive and assay. Once you've driven a Ford Escort sent over with a Mercury Tracer's driver's seat mistakenly installed, you begin to realize that they're barely in cahoots with themselves, much less the automotive press.

Another thing: I like trucks, and come from a long history of family SUVs. Counting aunts and uncles, there are more than 10 in my family alone. I own one, as do my sister and brother-in-law, and so do my parents, who added the first one (a 1985 Ford Bronco) to the family fleet just when I was able to drive and haven't been without one since. I know the SUV's limitations, their excesses, and in the dead of winter when the nearby hospital needs volunteers to transport people, their absolute usefulness.

Credentials? In the past 15 years, I've driven every edition of HUMMER vehicle, have gone through two courses of HUMMER driver training, and even managed to squeeze one into a compact parking spot at Louis Armstrong International Airport in New Orleans. I've chauffered my sister and husband from their wedding in a screaming-yellow H2, drawn the gaping stares of NASCAR fans at the summer Bristol race in a similarly screaming-yellow H1, and been deeper in Indiana mud in both of them than most would care to be. I've extracted other SUVs from Mayan ruins, Icelandic volcano tubes, and the infield of a Nebraska cloverleaf during a week-long, subzero trek across the upper Midwest.

And when it comes to HUMMERs, I'm generally in favor of them. The military vehicles have proven their worth in every scenario possible since they were deployed in the late 1980s. And even GM's H2 has its merits, though gas mileage is not among them. Exceeding its off-road capability requires spending at least 50 percent more on a new vehicle or accepting 50 percent less interior room, and even with its drinking problem, it's a manageable, surprisingly adept cruiser. More on that later. For many Americans the HUMMER brand conjures images of robber barons toasting away our future with oil martinis. For my money, HUMMER harmlessly telegraphs America–even though at present, it's not my personal choice for a daily driver. For the record, I'm pro-SUV, *laissez-faire* toward HUMMER, and a Log Cabin Republican who happens to own a Toyota Prius hybrid and a Honda Element sport-ute, both the most fuel-efficient vehicles in their class. Both by choice.

Finally, a little bit about naming. When AM General built its first High Mobility Multi-Wheeled Vehicle (HMMWV) the term was liberalized to "Humvee." When the company began to sell its vehicles to civilians, the "Hummer" nickname was applied to those vehicles (as it had been to the military vehicles). And GM's preference for its brand is HUMMER, caps theirs; the big AM General built vehicle is the HUMMER H1, and the GM-engineered SUV is the HUMMER H2. In this book, military vehicles will be referred to as Humvees; civilian versions in the 1990s will be Hummers; and GM-retailed vehicles will be HUMMERs.

Got it? Good. Let's drive.

Chapter 1

Birth of a Nation— of SUVs

Cruise the parking lot of any major American shopping center and it's easy to be overwhelmed—by the stray shopping carts, by the alarming increase in size of the American behind and the rapidly increasing numbers of beggars running a new panhandle in the parking lot: "The house that burned down last night, it was on TV news? That was mine."

Or you can be overwhelmed by the sheer numbers of SUVs. I park and, in the five spaces adjacent to mine, I count four sport-utes, all mid-size or larger. I also see the billboard for a Japanese company's new ute, looming larger than even City Hall across the street, and certainly better lit in these days of big state budget deficits.

But you don't expect to be overwhelmed by SUVs inside the bookstore. You expect cappuccino, left-leaning free newspapers, vividly hued local color and maybe, hidden behind the *Sopranos* DVD box set and note cards for every conceivable surgical occasion, the odd reference book. You get overwhelmed anyway.

"There's another book over there on how evil SUVs are if you're interested," says the clerk with the pierced chin as I poke around, trying to find some source material in a forest of multimedia.

Evil? Wait, can inanimate objects be evil? Or heroic? And while we're at it, how did we get here? How did America become the land of the sport-utility vehicle—and how did we get to the point where SUV owners are chastised for the type of vehicle they choose to drive?

None of those questions has an easy answer, but the long, glacial evolution of the sport-utility vehicle is nestled right in there with the rapid evolution of the automobile—a device that historian Daniel J. Boorstin called the "great equalizer" of the twentieth century. The automobile, he argued, meant that the poor man could go the same places as the rich man.

"The automobile has been an epoch-defining technology for the twentieth century," opines Kevin L. Borg, an assistant professor of history at James Madison University—and the rare academic with handy skills to fall back on, should JMU ever cease to be. Borg, an auto mechanic who went on to get a doctorate in technology history, says the automobile "started as a plaything for the rich and it's become the most ubiquitous piece of technology in American life." So the SUV is, like other automobiles, a bit player in the grand American experiment. But clearly, from its shape and its emergence in the late twentieth century, the SUV is different from the ordinary passenger car—and completely by the choice of those consumers who seek it out to differentiate themselves from the crowd. The SUV sets them apart: it makes them taller, better defended, more capable and more rugged than the average car and its driver.

But the SUV itself has undergone dramatic changes since it emerged from the primordial ooze of the last century. To be sure, SUVs haven't always offered DVD players, myriad cupholders, or exotic four-wheel-drive systems and other high-tech gadgets. In fact the very first SUVs had just one or two jobs in mind: carrying a load of horse manure to its drop target or hauling a zebra carcass back from the Serengeti to the lodge. Nowhere in the original mission statement for sport-utility vehicles did the mission include runs to McDonald's and Target.

They didn't even call them sport-utility vehicles when the first such vehicles were hybridized from trucks. Like some new organic variety of car (or like a virus, if you ask Arianna Huffington and other anti-SUV zealots), the SUV mutated from truck roots into various Internationals, Broncos and Suburbans, and Willys-Overlands. The vehicles were pressed into service in the dedicated niche where they fit: towing horse trailers, pounding the Kalahari in military missions, exploring the back forty on a family spread. And so they toiled peacefully for decades, with some unheralded variations like Hudson sportwagons and the odd Toyota Land Cruiser emerging from the stew of four-wheel-drive wagons.

But what makes a vehicle a sport-utility vehicle, anyway? Good question—and one that will take most of the rest of this chapter to answer.

What is an SUV?

If you think about it, some of the very first cars were SUV-like. They had to carry people and cargo and they had to go off-road—because there were no paved roads, only cobblestones and brick if drivers were lucky—and acres of fallow fields, fallen trees and mucky ruts when they weren't.

But there are some key distinctions between SUVs and ordinary passenger cars, and even the closely related station wagon. Psychologically, perhaps, the buyers couldn't be any more different—but when it comes to functionality, SUVs are essentially tall wagons with better ground clearance and some degree off-road capability.

You probably have your own ideas about what a sport-utility vehicle actually is, though. Lots of vehicles seem to claim to be SUVs or even sport-utility trucks (SUTs), a new spin on the SUV that covers anything with a bed and seats, from the former Chevy El Camino and lowly Subaru Brat, to the light-duty Honda SUT coming to market in 2006.

Someone or something has to have the ultimate say in what makes a vehicle a car or truck (and SUVs are classified as trucks). And in America's case it's the Department of Transportation and its subsidiary agency, the National Highway Traffic Safety Administration (NHTSA) that make up the ground rules.

The NHTSA defines what makes up trucks in a couple of different ways—and sport-utes depend on those definitions. While a passenger car is merely defined as "any four-wheel vehicle not designed for off-road use that is manufactured primarily for use in transporting 10 people or less," the definition of a truck is conditional. A truck, the NHTSA says, is a four-wheel vehicle designed for off-road operation—meaning it has four-wheel drive or has a gross vehicle weight of more than 6,000 pounds, or meets any one of five conditions: transporting more than 10 people; providing temporary living quarters; transporting property in an open bed; has more carrying capacity than passenger-carrying volume; or can be converted to an open-bed vehicle by removing the rear seat to form a flat, continuous floor with the use of simple tools.

By those definitions, the distinctions can be difficult. Ford's Explorer, for instance, was formerly a pure SUV, built from truck pieces and a wagon body and equipped with four-wheel drive. But what to call the later Explorer Sport Trac, an SUV-based vehicle with an exposed truck bed in back, but more passenger room than cargo room and not sold only with four-wheel drive? Or the Jeep Grand Cherokee, which has unibody construction and a smallish cargo area, but offers all-wheel drive? In the spectrum of sport-utility vehicles and wannabes, there are plenty of shades of grey.

The murkiest cases seem engineered to drive Ralph Nader nuts: Chrysler's five-door retro PT Cruiser wagon is ranked as a truck by the government—despite its tiny cargo area and front-wheel-drive format—because it offers a flat load floor, as does Honda's Element even though many versions don't even offer all-wheel drive. And for 2005, the new Subaru Outback lineup—including the four-door sedan—will be classified as a truck because the amount of space from the ground to the underside of the car is as tall as some trucks.

For the purposes of this book—and for some logical distinction—sport-utility vehicles will have a few defining characteristics. Here, they're generally based on trucks, have rear-wheel drive with available full-time four-wheel drive with a low gear, and a wagon body style suitable for carrying four or more people. For those newer car-based utility vehicles with front- or all-wheel drive and unibody construction (meaning the bodies are composed in box-like units, not built atop a set of frame rails as trucks are) we'll use the trendy term of "crossovers."

Neander-utes

Arguing which vehicle qualifies as the first sport-utility vehicle is as hazy a proposition as actually defining what makes a sport-utility vehicle. Even experts in the field give varying arguments.

A defining characteristic of SUVs, four-wheel drive, was still in its infancy through the first half of the century. Early electric vehicles technically were four-wheel drive, since some models had motors that spun each of their wheels. But four-wheel drive with conventional gas-engined cars was a different, more difficult technical prospect that lagged the first cars by at least a decade. (Four-wheel drive, for the previously uninterested, allows a vehicle to spread its power more evenly amongst its four wheels, which can give better traction on different driving surfaces and offer the potential to carry more payload. It uses a center differential to distribute the vehicle's power to all four wheels, and a low range gear to enable it to traverse the really nasty stuff. Systems without the low gear are generally referred to as having all-wheel drive.)

History tells us that Otto Zachow and William Besserdich built the first U.S.-made four-wheel-drive vehicle in 1911. Their Four Wheel Drive company supplied four-wheelers to the British and U.S. armies during the First World War, giving the technology a military presence that long outlived the actual pioneers and their company. In the years after the war, four-wheel-drive vehicles became more common, but most of those were Ford and Dodge station wagons converted to four-wheel drive after they were rolled off of the assembly line.

During the war, the four-wheel-drive vehicle most vividly etched into America's history came into use: the Jeep, made by Willys-Overland, a four-wheel-drive company at one time was the second-largest auto manufacturer in the U.S. Willys-Overland had won the contract to build the Jeep in a competition with Ford and the long since departed Bantam, and in doing so changed the course of its own history and America's, too. In short, the Jeep made the war effort work. So closely was it identified with the

American GI that its impact could be summed up in one cartoon—Pulitzer Prize-winning cartoonist Bill Mauldin's famously forlorn soldier being forced to shoot his Jeep, presumed to have given up after a heroic tour of duty. When it came home from war, the CJ Jeep became a staple of the off-road market—the single strand of DNA that would link today's Jeeps to their WWII heritage—and an icon, featured in exhibits in the Museum of Modern Art.

But was it a true SUV? Not by today's definition. Both the traditional Jeep and the modern-day reincarnation are two-door vehicles without much cargo storage, technically convertibles (though hard tops are an option on the Wrangler you can buy today) but also trucks by the Feds' rules. Part nostalgia piece, part ragtop, but not all SUV.

So what vehicle might have been the first sport-utility vehicle—a truck-based wagon built from the factory with four-wheel drive? Michael Davis, a member of the Automotive Press Association and the Society of Automotive Historians, a trustee of the National Automotive History Collection, an advisor to the Automotive Hall of Fame and a former public-relations executive at Ford Motor Company (whew!), casts a vote for the 1949 Jeep Station Wagon. While many point to the 1935-1936 Chevrolet Suburban wagons as the ur-SUVs, the truck-based vehicles didn't offer factory-installed four-wheel drive until 1957, according to Davis.

"I think the more likely contender was when the all-steel Jeep Station Wagon, first introduced in 1946, got 4WD in 1949," Davis says. "I pick the 1949 Jeep because it was four-wheel drive and more of a civilian-type vehicle, as opposed to a worker beast, and buyable at a Willys dealership right off the showroom floor, with no special order." Jeep advertised this vehicle as a "car," and a superior one to the station wagon because of its "all-steel body and top for greater safety and longer service" – a four-wheeler that was roomy,

HUMMER

The original concept for the GM HUMMER vehicle—a clear indicator of things to come.

smooth-riding and capable in the snow or rain, a classic definition that's withstood more than fifty years of progress.

Wagoneers fly, Eagles thud

And for half of that era of progress, SUVs weren't big business, they were small business. The classic American car was at its zenith in the 1950s and 1960s. Big sedans like the 1955 Chevrolet Bel Air and big convertibles like the 1959 Cadillac Eldorado ruled the roads and the iconography of America's highways: big, flashy, overly styled, and yet romantic in detail. Even in the 1960s, the emergence of the muscle car revved up the image of Detroit as the best car builders in the world. Trucks and sport-utes, by comparison, were a tiny portion of the country's market for new cars.

At least one company sensed the opportunity that the Jeep had opened, however. Still selling the war veteran in its showrooms, in 1953 Willys-Overland sold itself to Kaiser-Frazer to form the Kaiser-Jeep Corp. The move would trigger the next evolution of the sport-utility vehicle, and a move even closer to the spirit of today's SUVs.

The move came in the form of the Jeep Wagoneer. After months and millions of dollars of research, Kaiser-Jeep (which had ceased Willys car production in 1955 to focus on off-road vehicles) launched the Wagoneer in 1963 as the first luxurious off-road vehicle and the direct ancestor of today's full-size SUVs. It offered the first automatic transmission available with four-wheel drive, though rear-drive models offered it; two- and four-door versions were offered.

The Wagoneer seemed to contradict itself – it was a full-size wagon with the rugged heritage of Jeep underneath, from its four-wheel drive to its off-roadable frame, but also a comfortable ride, or so the ads went. One pictured the Wagoneer riding atop a rolled-out carpet across formidable rocks: "Try the new automatic transmission, power options, and quiet highway ride." It was the original application of the contradictory "luxury meets off-roading" mission that underpins every SUV costing more than $20,000 today.

That market positioning would allow Jeep to transcend its one-note war vehicle into a lineup of vehicles that would expand the notion of what a four-wheel-drive vehicle could be—and it would be copied endlessly by today's SUV brands pitching their wagons as the idea blend of off-road capability and luxury. Unique as the Wagoneer was, it couldn't keep Kaiser-Jeep independent forever. In 1970 American Motors bought the Jeep brand, allowing the Kaiser name to fade into history.

The buyer for Kaiser-Jeep might only have lived for thirty-four more years itself, but AMC's reputation for developing vehicles on the cheap is only exceeded by its legacy of midwifing the SUV through another set of labor pains. Even as it struggled financially through its last decade of corporate life, two of AMC's off-roaders—the Jeep Cherokee and the AMC Eagle—would be the precursors to the two of the most popular vehicle types on the market today.

American Motors was a composite of small brands that couldn't have much room to breathe in an era when General Motors controlled nearly 60 percent of the U.S. car market. Put together in the aftermath of World War II from the Nash and Hudson brands, left at the altar by Studebaker in an aborted merger, American Motors played the underdog role as it sold Ramblers and tried to innovate on the little cash it had. The fact that it was able to buy Kaiser-Jeep wasn't so much a statement of its strength, but of Kaiser-Jeep's sorry finances, despite the presence of the Wagoneer.

The Wagoneer proved successful enough that in 1974, Jeep split the lineup in two by adding the lower-cost Cherokee. Priced from a few hundred to nearly a thousand dollars less than the $6,000 Wagoneer, the Cherokee took on the role of the outdoor-exploration vehicle, even though its shared dimensions and profile of the four-door Wagoneer. The Wagoneer was free to move further upmarket. In 1984, when the company was a part of AMC, Jeep introduced a new Cherokee, dramatically smaller and lighter than the prior models – and perfectly timed to take advantage of the swelling SUV market. The Wagoneer/Cherokee nameplates lived on for nearly three decades each; the Wagoneer last sold in 1991 and the Cherokee was replaced in 2002 by the Jeep Liberty.

While Jeep pioneered the modern luxury SUV, the modern full-size SUV and the multi-SUV lineup, the company characteristically turned its financial hardships into motivation, budding another offshoot of the sport-ute family tree. The AMC Eagle, the dying breath of a never-great company, predated a whole generation of crossover vehicles, not to mention the entire Subaru Outback lineup and the newest Audi allroad vehicles. The model, which was sold from 1980 to 1987, was the first mass-produced four-wheel-drive car by an American company. Based on an older AMC car chassis, the Eagle came as a two-door, a four-door and as a wagon, all with a full-time four-wheel-drive system and more ground clearance (the measure from the ground to the underside of a vehicle's body) than the cosmetically similar AMC Concord. The Eagle was classified as a car for clean-air regulations, and despite its all-terrain capability, in all senses looked and felt like a passenger car –the hallmark of today's crossover vehicle. AMC sold more than 46,000 of them in the first year, but sales drifted downward along with the company's fortunes.

With all due respect to the dead, AMC had been poorly managed and cursed with homely vehicles. It was the runt of the American car litter. But the company had somehow channeled a startling amount of innovation through years of red ink. Its vehicles were twenty years ahead of their time for the kind of financial returns needed to keep the company afloat. By 1979, AMC had been forced to enter into a partnership with France's Renault to survive; Renault used the shell of AMC to build and market its own European-bred vehicles in the U.S. Renault eventually tired of the hassle of marketing to picky Americans who didn't want Euro-style sedans and jettisoned AMC after building a brand-new plant in Ontario to build its vehicles. In 1987, Renault sold its shares in AMC to Chrysler Corp., which took a new SUV project on the boards at AMC and used it to catapult the Jeep brand into thousands of garages in suburbia just five years later—and then, used Jeep to make itself an attractive target for an international takeover rife with intrigue.

CAFE society

Detroit deeply wounded itself in the late 1960s and early 1970s by not taking its competition seriously. A clutch of German and Japanese brands—Toyota, Honda and VW—had landed on American shores with fuel-efficient compact cars that gradually built a big audience with buyers on both coasts. And then the oil shocks hit: war in the Middle East and embargoes from the countries controlling America's imported oil supplies halted shipments, starving the country of gasoline at a time when Detroit's biggest passenger cars and wagons barely could muster 12 miles to the gallon.

Even before the embargoes, America's opinion of the car world was changing. For fifty years a symbol of progress, the car culture was beginning to backfire. Traffic choked off cities with smog, while the exodus to the suburbs made possible by cars had stripped some cities (particularly Detroit) clean of entire prosperous neighborhoods, leaving empty homes and businesses in their wake and decimated tax bases.

Cars like the Volkswagen Beetle typified a new market Americans were ready for: the inexpensive, fuel-efficient city car.

Freedom and mobility still defined the American dream— but the consequences of cars on the environment and cities were tempering enthusiasm for traditional American iron and unchecked consumption.

And in response to the gas crises, the government set out to mandate how much gas cars and trucks could consume without penalty. The new CAFE (Corporate Average Fuel Economy) rules finished off Detroit's full-size cars and wagons and handed more fuel-efficient imported vehicles an unchallenged beachhead.

First enacted by Congress in 1975, CAFE's express purpose was to reduce energy consumption by increasing the fuel economy of cars and light trucks. According to the rules set up in 1975, manufacturers would have to meet an average fuel economy for all the vehicles they sold, with an overall goal of boosting car mileage to 27.5 mpg by 1985.

Trucks, however, were to be defined differently from passenger cars according to the rules outlined earlier in this chapter. And they would be allowed to meet a lighter fuel-economy standard, one that eventually reached 20.7 mpg in 1996. Light trucks that exceed 8,500 pounds in gross vehicle weight rating (GVWR) don't have to comply with either CAFE standard. Mostly, these vehicles include pickup trucks, sport-utility vehicles and large vans.

Why did the government classify trucks separately from passenger cars? In the mid-1970s, trucks didn't take nearly as large a percentage of the automobile market as today—it was 20 percent in 1975, versus more than 50 percent in 2003. Dr. Jeffrey Runge, the current head of the NHTSA, says that when the CAFE legislation was passed in 1975, "light trucks played a different role both in society and in the vehicle market. Light trucks made up only 20 percent of the America's vehicles and were used primarily as work vehicles, hauling lumber, farming equipment, and small business materials. Today, light trucks make up more than 50 percent of all vehicles sold and are used not only as work vehicles but increasingly, largely due to the proliferation of SUVs, as passenger vehicles, to haul children and groceries. This increase accounts for much of the decline in the fuel economy of new fleets and contributes to our growing dependence on oil imports."

During the 1990s the CAFE rules were frozen, but the standards had been planned for increases that came into being in March of 2003. While leaving car rules at 27.5 mpg, the NHTSA issued new light truck standards, setting a standard of 21.0 mpg for model-year 2005, 21.6 mpg for 2006, and 22.2 mpg for 2007.

CAFE took away Detroit's very identity, and it would take more than two decades of engineering toil and a computer revolution for General Motors and Ford to regain their footing. And while already efficient fleets of Japanese cars were flooding the market, American companies spent hundreds of millions of dollars trying to retool their most famous nameplates to meet the new rules. Ford's Thunderbird lost a thousand pounds when it re-emerged post-CAFE in 1977. The Mustang had already been gelded, and shared most of its mechanicals with the lowly CAFE-pleasing Pinto. And those were among the finer efforts possible in the age before the microchip made emissions easy and boosted horsepower in today's four-cylinders to match that of some of yesterday's V-8s. Other attempts to meet CAFE were utter disasters, like GM's experiments with variable-displacement and diesel engines. Meanwhile, Japanese manufacturers had entered the U.S. market with smaller, more fuel-efficient vehicles common in their home market, and easily kept pace with the new regulations.

The answer lay in trucks. From the moment the CAFE system was inaugurated, it became the best, most profitable interest of carmakers—particularly America automakers, fluent in crafting big vehicles powered by equally big V-8 engines—to build vehicles that qualified as trucks. The loophole constructed by Congress would take fifteen years to make its full size evident, but it legally gave companies a way to avoid the tougher CAFE burden while meeting the seemingly insatiable American demand for bigger vehicles.

Other critics suggest some evildoing on the part of automakers in taking advantage of the loophole—pushing trucks though they are by some measures less safe for inexperienced drivers—but it's hard to overlook CAFE's own flaws and not assign it full responsibility for record automotive oil consumption. CAFE is like telling an American family that the teenagers can only eat 1,000 calories a day and the parents, 1,500. Someone's going to go hungry—unless you start calling the kids adults and charging them rent.

"The fuel standards meant the end of the big, V-8 family station wagon because it was a gas hog, and it was classified as a family car, so the standards applied to it," reminds Professor Borg. "The blind spot was not seeing that the light truck market could replace the station wagon."

CAFE made the case, and other taxes already on the books gave Detroit the upper hand in building and selling trucks. The so-called "chicken tax" charges a 25-percent tariff on trucks imported into the U.S., and for decades made it financially impossible for foreign companies to compete against domestic offerings—unless they built trucks in America, of course. Until that day came, American truckmakers could exploit their advantage in building vehicles that would suit the American landscape—big vehicles with big payloads, effortless V-8 engines and durable live-axle designs with four-wheel drive.

Not much has changed in principle for CAFE since the original legislation—only minor tweaks to truck economy, in fact. But several attempts have been made on its life, and even more attempts have been made to drastically increase the mandated fuel-economy numbers for both trucks and cars. The 1990 Bryan Bill tried to boost the numbers to 40 mpg for the nation's fleet of passenger cars and was gunned down by a single vote (or, depending on your political leanings, by the profuse lobbying efforts of Detroit).

Nearly thirty years of hindsight has shown even the Feds that CAFE, has backfired. "It is clear that the downsizing of vehicles that occurred during the first decade of the CAFE program had serious safety consequences," said a June 2003 report by the National Highway Traffic Safety Administration.

"Back when these regulations were written, no one thought of a minivan. There were no SUVs. And it wouldn't have been fair to tell a Jeep driver that they had to conform to the same standards (of a passenger car)," said Hurd. "Who would have thought that there would be Cadillac pickups and SUVs?" NHTSA spokesman Tim Hurd asks.

Against that backdrop, automakers and consumers took a while to find the way around the rules. But for companies already more versed in building trucks, the SUV phenomenon came naturally—and quickly.

The explosion: Ford Explorer and Jeep Grand Cherokee

A host of sport-utility vehicles had evolved from trucks throughout the 1970s and 1980s—vehicles like the Dodge Ramcharger, Ford Bronco, Chevrolet Blazer, both the full-size version and the later mid-sizer, and the Chevrolet Suburban, not to mention the Land Rover, Range Rover, and Toyota Land Cruiser. And already, the boasting of SUV prowess had worked its way into the marketing of vehicles that had only sold about 35,000 vehicles

Birth of a Nation—of SUVs

The U.S. Border Patrol commissioned a set of white Humvees to be used along the Mexican border.

in 1964—but twice as many in 1970. Ford's Bronco was pitched by Ford General Manager Donald Frey "as neither car nor truck, but a vehicle which combines the best of both worlds. The Bronco can serve as a family sedan, sports roadster, snowplow or farm and civil defense vehicle. It has been designed to go nearly anywhere and do nearly anything."

But it wasn't until 1990 that a runaway sales success emerged from what had been, until then, a niche market in the U.S. It might have been a Jeep vehicle, if financial turmoil hadn't ended in the Jeep brand being absorbed into Chrysler Corp. and set back the timing of their mid-size SUV by a few years. Instead the most popular SUV to date came from the Ford Motor Company, and the American automotive landscape hasn't looked the same since.

Ford had been working on a wagon built from its compact truck platform and to replace the recall- and rollover-prone Bronco II. Introduced in 1983 as a 1984 model, the two-door Bronco II shared its running gear with the smaller Ranger pickup truck. When it came time to redo the vehicle, executives in charge of the program decided it was time to add a four-door model to the lineup and target buyers left in the station-wagon void.

The Ford Explorer arrived in 1990 as a 1991 model and promptly changed the American car market forever. Available in two-door or four-door form, the Explorer was the SUV, fully actualized at a popular price point (four-doors started at less than $17,500). It offered truck capability wrapped in a stylish wagon body and filled with car features: plush carpeting and lighted vanity mirrors were mated with four-wheel drive and big trailer-towing capacity. A hit from the day it went on sale, the Explorer became the workhorse of suburbia, shuttling kids and groceries and possibly going off-road by the loosest of definitions—

and skirting the issue of higher fuel-economy averages by virtue of its truck heritage.

Five years before, the 1986 Taurus had turned around Ford's lackluster financial condition by showing that American cars could compete dynamically and stylistically with the mid-size imports. The Explorer wasn't as large a critical success but its sales rivaled that of the Taurus at a higher per-vehicle profit. With the Explorer, Ford had stumbled on a magic formula of space, functionality and good looks that would pull even more passenger-car buyers from those ranks and put them into higher-profit trucks.

Just three months after it was introduced the Explorer was the best selling mid-size SUV. Within ten years the Explorer would replace the Taurus as the company's best-selling mid-size passenger vehicle—and would also be a part of the company's most embarrassing recall spectacle since the Pinto implosion of the 1970s.

The other pillar of the explosive growth of SUVs was the Jeep Grand Cherokee. Though American Motors already had begun work on what would become the Jeep Grand Cherokee, really the first modern mid-size SUV, the collapse of AMC and its absorption into the Chrysler Corp. prevented it from hitting the market until 1992. But the Grand Cherokee was an equally savvy take on the truck heritage of the brand, blended deftly with passenger-car comforts. In fact, unlike the Explorer's truck-based frame, the Grand Cherokee was built in the way cars were – in boxlike sections welded together called a unibody.

Effectively, the Explorer and the Grand Cherokee set the stage for both companies' prosperity in the early 1990s, surely saving Chrysler from another bankruptcy and propelling Ford's market share to a point where analysts questioned whether it would one day overtake General Motors as the biggest car company in the world.

The big bang

Every analyst and every critic has a theory as to why SUVs went from being rare sights on the Interstates to the vehicle of choice of one out of every four car-buying Americans. They're probably all right, to some degree, but three major factors played the biggest roles in the growing dominance of the sport-ute.

Chief among them was government regulation, mostly the CAFE rules. CAFE has had a double-barrel effect on automakers. Since 1983, manufacturers have paid more than $500 million in civil penalties. But it's the long-term dent it's put in Detroit's door panels that has helped imports garner more than 30 percent of the U.S. market. While Europe and Japan were building small cars that were poised to do well under CAFE, American carmakers were building big American cars more suited to U.S. roads and lifestyles and tastes of the time. Engineering cars up in size to American taste while meeting CAFE would prove to be much easier than chopping down Detroit's biggest land yachts into CAFE-sized pieces. The answer at the time might have been old-fashioned European subsidies to help Detroit hobble through the 1970s and 1980s while developing a new generation of more fuel-efficient vehicles, which could have limited the need to turn to trucks.

Technology can only influence society to a certain degree. To some extent we're just animals reproducing to survive, and that biological imperative is the second big factor in the growth of SUVs— the growth of America in population. Coupled with vast tides of legal and illegal immigrants, America entered an "Echo Boom" in the 1980s and 1990s that fueled a need for larger family vehicles. Baby Boomers were growing up and having families, and as a result, live births hit a three-decade peak in 1990, when 4.2 million babies were born—only 110,000 fewer than the baby boom's peak in 1961. Between 1978 and 2001, America recorded 78.2 million births, a higher overall total than the 74.9 million births credited to the original 1946-1964 Baby Boom. The minivan, which Chrysler pioneered in 1984, took the first wave of families under its wing—and when the minivan image soured, it was the SUV that took up the slack.

The third major reason isn't so easily quantified as it is observed. With the start of the 1980s, America seemed finally ready to shed the cultural malaise of the 1970s—Vietnam, the Carter administration, stagflation, oil embargoes and Iranian hostages. The election of Ronald Reagan augured in a new sense of patriotism and national pride that the Hollywood actor turned governor turned leader of the free world proved to be particularly adept in channeling. Pride in being American had overtaken the White House and quickly transferred to the automotive realm, and the appearance of two great sport-utes from America's heartland could not have hurt their popularity—nor could have the coincidental disappearance of some of Ford and GM's last big rear-drive wagons, the Olds Custom Cruiser and Ford Country Squire. Though GM would hold out with its Caprice station wagon for a few years more, the ranks of American station wagons had been decimated and downsized into near-oblivion—and SUVs were a timely successor in a time of revisited American patriotism.

Whatever the cause, lawmakers and carmakers never foresaw the big boom in SUVs that came in 1990. Within a decade, one in every six vehicles sold in the U.S. was a sport-utility vehicle. Light trucks went from 20 percent of the market in 1980 to nearly 52 percent of the market, due in large part to poorly conceived legislation. "SUVs caught everyone by surprise," says Walter McManus, an automotive analyst with J.D. Power and Associates, a California-based marketing research firm.

More figures indicate the growth of SUVs wasn't so much rapid as explosive. In 1980, SUV sales ranged at about 200,248, or 1.8 percent of the U.S. market. By 2002 the number had ballooned to 4.21 million vehicles, or 20 percent of the U.S. market. Folded in with pickup and other light trucks, in 1980 the truck market numbered 2.23 million sales or 19.9 percent—while in 2002 it had overtaken cars with 8.7 million trucks sold, or 51.8 percent of the market.

SUVs had made it big, and it paid to add trucks to lineups that had no truck heritage whatsoever. Even brands with no off-road heritage—Acura, Lincoln, Cadillac, Lexus, an even Porsche—got into the game primarily because of profit. The average SUV, according to some estimates, booked $5000 or much more in profit for the car company selling it, versus $500 or even much less for the average passenger car. Without needing an explanation, Acura MDXs, Caddy Escalades and Lincoln Navigators became the norm.

SUVs had become objects of affluence. In 1990, none of the vehicles that cost more than $25,000 were trucks. By 2000, of those costing $25,000 (inflation-adjusted to $35,000), the majority were trucks and SUVs.

Of course, some still toiled away at their original and intended duties: a small company named AM General began making military vehicles for the Army, and some SUVs stuck by their off-road roots as long as they could, the big Ford Broncos and Chevy Blazers chief among them.

Why the SUV?

The biggest question is, why? Given the option of buying something more space- and fuel-efficient than an SUV—which most minivans are—why would otherwise rational people choose a sport-utility vehicle?

Certainly there were politically influenced reasons, but CAFE and other legislation only enabled the truck and SUV market to explode. It would take a nation of buyers to decide that the tradeoffs in gas mileage and comfort were worth the off-road, all-weather and towing capability.

That's not a difficult stretch to imagine for most shoppers, Borg argues. "People buy cars based not on what their usual operations are but what the extreme uses are," he says "The new prosperity and the ubiquity of the two-income household meant the second vehicle could be a utility-type vehicle."

In the case of the SUV, it's about what's promised, in marketing come-ons, in looks and in action. Taken to the most esoteric, anthropological levels, SUVs are about superiority. Instantly distinguishable from both cars and trucks, they are bigger and more capable than station wagons with which they share most of their DNA. They are not egalitarian. They are not democratic. They are a challenge to you and to the car-driving society around them, according to some of the very people Detroit firms hire to figure out how best to appeal to the SUV buyer.

Dr. Clothaire Rapaille is probably the most controversial theorist among these men. Born in Vichy France educated as a psychologist, and author of *Seven Secrets of Marketing in a Multi-Cultural World,* Rapaille consults with car companies to help them identify untapped markets for new kinds of cars, as well as trying to steer the associations shoppers make with certain brands and vehicles.

Rapaille believes safety and security are the dominant forces at work in the SUV boom. The purchase of an SUV is a "reptilian" response to perceived threats to one's well-being, he theorized in *Fortune* Magazine in 2002. "One aspect of the reptilian is survival," he told writer Phil Patton. "That is why people run out to buy guns—even though you can't shoot down a plane with a gun—or sneakers to run fast, or a big powerful SUV."

The desire to stay alive begets the desire to reproduce, too—and in that respect the SUV also serves as a symbol to attract suitable mates, he believes. "In addition to the survival aspect of the reptilian,"

HUMMER

Camouflage is one of the color options on the civilian HUMMER.

he adds, "there is the reproductive aspect. The desire to reproduce—to get the girls."

Other analysts are grounded in a more tangible realm. Timothy Malefyt is one of those theorists. Holder of a doctorate in anthropology from Brown University, Malefyt's the "Director of Cultural Discoveries" at advertising giant BBDO and the author of *Advertising Cultures*, a study of the connection between advertising and anthropology. Malefyt helped with the turnaround of the Cadillac brand and with the introduction of the Escalade SUV in particular, and it's his contention that the SUV is the current-day symbol for power on the American road.

In general, automobiles are "great metaphors for how we portray ourselves to others," he says. And that's beginning to make itself known in the resurgence of dramatic, highly stylized car design. The big grille is back, as witnessed on new cars like the Chrysler 300C and Audi A8, he reasons. "It's saying 'watch out.'"

When it comes to SUVs, people identify with an image unlike that of station wagons, Malefyt believes. "The concept or metaphor of the wagon was always the wagon train—not the bronco, the cowboy, not the leader but the settlers, those more vulnerable. It doesn't project a sense of leadership."

And while minivans were at first unconventional vehicles without labels, the mass adoption by families gave the vehicles possibly the most deadly stereotype in today's car business. "Through use, it was the connection with 'soccer Moms' that just killed it." For parents eager to avoid getting old and responsible, the soccer-mom tag "is the reinvention of their mom – she gives in her identity in a sense for those of her kids."

SUV buyers are psychologically different, he believes. They're hesitant to give in their lives for those of their children altogether, even though they're schlepping kids, settling down, and becoming parents. "They don't want a wagon that's about following," Malefyt says. "Blazer, Bronco TrailBlazer – that's the metaphor they want. Active, dynamic and powerful."

And they don't necessarily want to share, either. While minivan shoppers see their vehicles as the embodiment of the community–picking up carpools at daycare, for example—SUV buyers want to be away from contact from other people, Malefyt thinks. "People have taken on a whole other attitude as drivers. It's almost a new form of communicating – distancing themselves from each other. The reality of driving today is doing anything you can do to ward other people off." It's rooted, he thinks, in the very earliest days of the country, when colonists said, "don't tread on me" to the imperial powers in England.

That's why the SUV has channeled impulses that maybe weren't tapped 20 years ago—or possibly didn't even exist. "Americans are tied to tradition very well. Twenty years ago, the sportscar was symbol of sexiness. Now it's about power. SUVs like the HUMMER are the new image of what America is about—the new cowboys."

Chapter 2

A HUMMER Is Born

"That creaking you hear is normal," my driving instructor Pete tells me as we slide from one boulder to the next, using the tires of the truck to knuckle our way down stairs made out of rock and liberally coated with mud. The HUMMER expert beside me, I've decided, is my only chance to keep from pranging the sides of the nearly new H1 I'm piloting into non-factory-authorized origami.

When you're driving someone else's $110,000 SUV into deeply unfamiliar Indiana muck it pays to listen—and when Pete tells me to slam it into the deep mud rut ahead and never mind the creaking, I obey.

I also get stuck in window-high mud. I wait for a tow strap and the HUMMER ahead to yank me free. I am muddy and discouraged—but not as muddy as Pete, who gets paid to teach civilian HUMMER owners and Special Ops military alike how to use their new toys. While I inspect the controls and try to look like I should be inside at the wheel instead of hip-deep in the slop, he's outside knee-deep into the muck, wiping spots of dirt from his glasses, way past his sorely need cigarette break.

Once we're free, we return to the campus that sits inside the test track that used to prove out new Studebakers when that brand still built new vehicles more than 40 years ago. It's a small infield, home to a corrugated-steel warehouse just getting its own neighboring picnic pavilion, landscaping and irrigation—pretty prosaic digs for an affiliate of the vast multibillion-dollar GM empire. But like the Humvees that transport the U.S. military and the HUMMERs that promise the best off-road capability on earth, every part of the infield serves a purpose. It begins and end with the test courses AM General has built to challenge every aspect of the HUMMERs' expertise: staggered dirt moguls for the trucks' suspension to navigate, deep standing water to be forded, and vertical obstacles to be clawed up and over.

Four of us civilians are learning the ins and outs of HUMMER driving—but we're not alone. Across the infield, a crew of Special Ops military is training for a mission we're not allowed to know. But the servicemen are allowed to take us around in the military-spec Humvees they're being taught to drive and repair.

"Just don't ask them what the mission is," requests one of the other instructors. "They can't tell you."

And so it goes on an average blustery-cold day at the HUMMER Driving Academy, which for owners paying $5,250 for the privilege, gives the deepest dive and best instruction on how to actually use their precision military tool. Along with the requisite factory tour, compass and GPS instruction, and armloads of HUMMER schwag, the well-heeled owners drive away with expert instruction in recovery techniques (not the 12-step kind) and advice on what kinds of off-road gear to purchase for their own adventures. HUMMERs are born here—on the outer fringe of South Bend, not too far from Touchdown Jesus and the Notre Dame campus—and so are HUMMER drivers.

How HUMMER got here is even more compelling a story than the evolution of the SUV itself. Fold in all the drama and downward spirals of the automobile industry—and then stir in the world-changing victories of the U.S. military and the feast-or-famine supporting role played by the companies that outfit our fighting men and women.

It all began here in a corner of Indiana known more for industrial blight than engineering might—but what emerged has built a reputation for ingenuity and durability that some might have thought had disappeared from America. In the 1960s, when Studebaker went out of business, they sold off the worthwhile chunks of the empire piecemeal. The factory and its land, and the nearby hunting grounds, went along with a contract to build military vehicles for the Army. And some 30 years later, it would be the birthplace of the first HMMWV—the generic name for what would become the instantly identifiable, world-beating Humvee.

Come together

At its roots, HUMMER is a descendant of good heartland stock—the kind of utilitarian forebears that built America up from its agrarian roots. Its story is a humble one, and like the history of the SUV, the first seventy years of HUMMER are largely the story of the consolidation of the U.S. auto industry. Before World War II, automakers literally could be found across the country; Detroit was the center of the industry, but there were other companies based in New York, Baltimore, even northern Indiana.

The earliest off-roaders owed as much to prosaic beginnings and ingenious tinkering as did the automobile. In 1903, the

Standard Wheel Company of Terre Haute, Indiana, began building cars to go along with its bicycles by introducing the first Overland "Runabout" model. Within five years, the company was sold as the auto industry began to implode on themselves in advance of the Great Depression: Overland went to John North Willys, who moved the operations to Toledo and formed the Willys-Overland Company in 1912. The company's first bankruptcy came early, but after the Depression, Willys-Overland Motors, Inc. was re-formed.

With the advent of World War I, four-wheel-drive technology found its first killer app—as the ideal drivetrain for vehicles that carried troops to the most remote battlefields, whether they were lined with mud, strewn with boulders, or swept with sand. Proven out during the Great War and critical to the postwar efforts around the war theater, particularly in the Middle East, four-wheelers were still being built the old-fashioned way: existing trucks were bought and converted by other companies with military contracts. Marmon-Herrington held one such contract, and began modifying trucks into four-wheel-drive military vehicles that would be used to service an oil pipeline contract in Mesopotamia, or modern-day Iraq.

The early four-wheel-drive vehicles had enormous virtue, enabling troop and cargo transport into areas that were more difficult to supply and man by other means. But they were far from perfect. The technology needed another round of development. One of the problems of these early designs was rapid tire wear, caused by the lack of a center differential. But that technology and the coming of another World War would lead to innovation, and would propel the off-roader to a legendary spot in the American psyche. In the 1940s, in support of the war effort, Willys-Overland built more than 360,000 of the new "jeep" 4x4s for military use and made a contribution to the war effort equally as important as the bombers built in Ford factories and the individual contributions of the millions of soldiers who served and died during the war. The Jeep became the visual equivalent of the U.S. military's might, so much so that despite its drawbacks as a passenger vehicle, thousands were sold in the postwar era through Willys dealers.

Willys' Jeep fortunes wouldn't last. Like other smaller automotive brands, the hurdles of modernization and the economic shutdown imposed on the nation during the world war (other than military contracts, that is) were too much to bear. By wartime, the market had shrunk largely to a dozen or two independent major carmakers, and soon would plummet to a handful as the post-war economic boom turned into the recession of the early 1950s. In that decade the smaller independent American car companies began huddling with each other to buffer themselves against the monolithic General Motors, which controlled something near 60 percent of the market by the early 1960s, and to a lesser extent Ford and Chrysler. In April 1953 Willys-Overland Motors, Inc. was purchased by Henry J. Kaiser, who ran it as Willys Motors for a decade before changing the name to Kaiser-Jeep Corporation in 1963.

Studebaker was a another good example of the boom-and-bust climate: after the war, many car companies were slow to ramp up new models, but Studebaker was among the first to market and for a while, it flourished. But the company's difficulties returned swiftly. The company went out of business in 1964 and its leftovers—including a contract to build military vehicles and its headquarters in South Bend, Ind.—were absorbed into Kaiser-Jeep.

Kaiser-Jeep operated at a profit, but the consolidation momentum was too strong. Few Kaiser passenger cars were visible on America's highways, but because of military contracts like that to build the second-generation M151 "Jeep," as well as its burgeoning Jeep brand business, Kaiser was an attractive takeover target. And in 1970, it was indeed taken over, by the American

HUMMER

AM General's assembly lines for both the military Humvees and the HUMMER H2 share space in Mishawaka, a neighbor to South Bend, Ind.

Motors Corporation, itself an amalgam of the old Nash and Hudson brands.

When it purchased Kaiser-Jeep, AMC shut down the Kaiser car operations, and split the company into two logical pieces: the Commercial Products Division in Toledo, which would be called Jeep Corporation, and the Government Products Division, headquartered in South Bend, Ind. In 1971, the Government Products Division was spun off to become a separate, wholly owned subsidiary of American Motors known as AM General Corporation.

As AM General built out the rest of the Studebaker and other contracts, the situation at AMC went from difficult to dire. To quickly acquire a new range of cars to sell, AMC agreed to sell Renault's European-bred vehicles in its U.S. dealerships; Renault infused $135 million into the company and bought 5 percent of its stock. AMC needed still more investment but before Renault could up its stake in AMC to 46.4 percent, the company would have to shed its military contract business before the U.S. government would approve Renault's controlling interest in AMC. In 1983 AM General was sold to LTV Corporation, paving the way for a deeper Renault/AMC alliance.

But the alliance would end abruptly and without profit. In 1987 Renault/AMC was dissolved and the best assets of the partnership—the Jeep brand and a new plant in Ontario, near Toronto—were sold to the Chrysler Corporation. Jeep, a distant cousin of AM General's, would later be a part of the global conglomerate formed when Daimler-Benz merged with (many say took over) Chrysler Corp. in 1998, a trans-Atlantic deal that later grafted on a controlling stake in Japan's Mitsubishi Motors and a significant investment in South Korea's Hyundai.

The hundreds of brands making up the automotive landscape in the U.S. at the turn of the twentieth century had boiled down to

General Motors and Ford, plus Chrysler Group as a part of DaimlerChrysler. AM General was a seeming relic of the old ways of the auto industry, left to fend for itself on military contracts alone.

The competition begins

AM General wasn't building anything particularly exotic when proposals began circulating for a new type of military vehicle— a so-called High Mobility Multi-Purpose Wheeled Vehicle, HMMWV by its requisite military acronym. The company, led by Jim Armour, an ex-Ford executive who joined AMC in 1972 and migrated into the AM General business, had been fulfilling old contracts to build second-generation Jeeps, postal vehicles and military versions of pickup trucks. AM General hadn't built any new vehicles, hadn't engineered anything from the ground up, and had no experience in fielding new work for the Pentagon—only in maintaining the money already flowing into the company.

By this time, the military Jeep had gone through many iterations—and through the Vietnam War, the "Jeeps" used were actually M151 vehicles, largely developed and sold to the government by Ford Motor Company, although some were produced under contract by Kaiser-Jeep and later, AM General. Those M151 MUTTs (Military Utility Tactical Truck) weren't known as the best vehicles to drive: they were less durable at first, though later design changes made them more reliable, but worse they could be difficult to control for untrained drivers.

In the mid-1970s, the Pentagon approached its contractors to submit prototypes for a new vehicle that would replace a fleet of then-existing vehicles. The original mission for these prototypes would be to replace the existing "jeep" and a range of other trucks used mainly for cargo and troop transport, as well as mobile missile launchers and telecommunications outposts. They needed to be transportable as well, capable of being carried by helicopters or stuffed into cargo planes.

While companies began submitting prototypes for the competition—including Chrysler Defense and Teledyne—the mission for the new range of vehicles grew. In the name of efficiency, the military specs for the new HMMWV were expanded: not only would the program vehicles replace the M151 quarter-ton utility vehicles, they would also replace M274 1/2-ton mules, the M561 1/2-ton Gama Goat troop carriers, and the M880 1/4-ton pickup trucks.

The initial specs for the competition would be delivered to interested bidders in 1979. The specs would define a vehicle that would be the most versatile military vehicle to date. The HMMWV would have to be able to "shoot and scoot," to carry munitions from machine guns to TOW missiles and to have enough power to use them sparingly. The Pentagon estimated that the vehicle would spend 40 percent of its time off road, 30 percent on the highway and 30 percent on smaller roads. And as a result of its support role, the HMMWV also had to be fast enough to keep up with the new generation of M1 Abrams tanks and the Bradley fighting vehicles for which it would play a support role.

The versatility of the HMMWV would have to extend to its driving capability. The specs required the vehicle to be able to go up a 60-percent incline (not a 60-degree, which would be closing in on vertical), and traverse a 40-percent side grade. And when it came to rolling over off-road obstacles, the HMMWV would have few rivals if any: the 72-degree approach angle and 37.5-degree departure angle meant that the HMMWV could climb steep rocks without much worry of damaging the front or rear ends.

And as a troop and cargo carrier, it would have to be able to transport 2,500 pounds of payload, with a gross vehicle weight of

8,660 pounds. Maximum curb weight was set at 5,200 pounds; towing capacity would be 3,400 pounds.

Originally AM General had no intention to bid on the project, partly because of the expense involved and because of its relative lack of experience. But when another contractor, the Texas-based company FMC, approached AM General about contract manufacturing the new HMMWV, Armour and company reconsidered. The decision to reconsider would nearly break the company financially, but it would also make its products a household name around the world.

In 1979, AM General commenced work on its proposed HMMWV. The lack of experience in designing military vehicles had worked in AM General's favor. Rather than recycling bits from older vehicles, it had created a design with an entirely new ladder-frame vehicle originally powered by a diesel engine, but quickly switched to a General Motors V-8 diesel with a three-speed automatic—a powertrain found in other Army vehicles, which led to more commonality with repair parts and the fuel used at the front. By February the company had built pilot vehicles and logged more than 17,000 miles of testing.

After 11 months of work researching and developing its ideas for the new-generation military vehicle, AM General took its HMMWV prototypes to the Nevada desert in July 1980 for testing that would duplicate the Pentagon tests to come. More than doing its homework, AM General was ensuring that its vehicle wouldn't just meet the HMMWV specifications but would exceed them.

In February 1981 the military's motor pool—TACOM, or Tank Automotive and Armor Command—had issued the final specs for XM998, the HMMWV vehicle. Out of 61 invitations sent to bid on the project, three companies were picked to enter the testing trials: Teledyne, Chrysler Corporation's defense arm (later General Dynamics), and AM General. In June 1981, the Army gave prototype contracts to the three companies with the assignment to take their prototypes to the next level. Each company would have to develop TOW missile carriers, cargo and troop carriers, and ambulance variants for the competition. Eleven prototypes would have to be delivered to for testing by May 1982.

Additional specs included a top speed of more than 60 mph, a driving range of 300 miles or more, and ballistic protection for a 16-gram fragment hitting the vehicle at 225 meters per second. In terms of dimensions, the next round of vehicles would have to be 85 inches wide at most, 195 inches long at most, and 69 inches tall or less.

The dimensions were critical, since the HMMWV would have to be stored in military aircraft and dropped into a combat zones with no more than half the vehicles lost in the process—dropped from a plane traveling at 200 mph at 15 feet above the ground, that is. (In action, Humvees can land 300 feet down the airfield once dropped from cargo planes).

Of the three companies bidding in the final round with prototypes, AM General was the first to complete its test vehicles. The prototypes were delivered to Army test grounds in Aberdeen, Md., and Yuma, Ariz., in April 1982 and later, to Fort Hunter-Riggett in California in September 1982. During a five-month test, the AM General vehicles were the first to complete durability testing, were the lightest vehicles in the test and the best performers.

But they weren't the cheapest. One of the proposals came in a good $2,000 cheaper per vehicle than the others. AM General's own HMMWV prototypes were $2000 per vehicle above the low bid, but by their own estimates, offered more bang for the buck. The cost advantage of the other entry disappeared when AM General's lifecycle costs were factored in, according to the company's engineers.

In a first for military contracting, the HMMWV contract didn't go to the company with the cheapest bid. The Pentagon awarded AM General the HMMWV contract on its merit on March 22, 1983. What was to be the first of many production contracts called for 55,000 vehicles to be delivered to the U.S. Government over a five-year period. By completion of the contract in 1989, options could raise the number of vehicles to 70,000. AM General had come from behind to win TACOM's confidence, though it hadn't built a newly designed vehicle of its own.

What is a Humvee?

AM General's win in the HMMWV derby had come through ingenuity and sound, ground-up engineering. The HMMWV–already murderized into "Humvee"–would be a flexible vehicle planned as a family of five models in 15 different configurations, all based on a common set of mechanicals. It's the Swiss Army knife of the American military–or more imaginatively, the military's Ferrari, purpose-built with little concern for convenience and all its expertise devoted to specific capabilities.

The models would include the M998 Cargo/Troop Carrier–the Army's family wagon; the M966 TOW (Tube-launched, Optically-sighted, Wire-guided) missile carrier; the M1025/1027/1043/1044 armament carrier, similar to the TOW model but with different armaments, including grenade launchers and machine guns; the M1037 tactical command vehicle; and the M1035/M996/M997 ambulances.

Most Humvees are configured as wagons, but differences exist between the vehicles made for different purposes. The special body style required by the TOW missile carrier–a "fastback" design–doesn't carry more cargo. It's sloped because the back blast from the missile would rip the roof off a standard Humvee. The communications antenna has its own shield to prevent it from being blown off, too. Communications vehicles have increased payloads for carrying tons of equipment used to link up cell phone networks and radar terminals. And ambulances, one of the most expensive models, are fitted with larger wagon backs to haul the wounded to safety

Some models are specialized for singularly unique missions. Humvees are currently deployed in conjunction with the air defense in Washington, D.C., protecting the Pentagon, outfitted with Stinger missiles and machine guns and smoke generators. There's even a "Humvee on Mars"—a special vehicle sent to the Mars Institute at NASA's Devon Island, N.C., facility, and used to study mobility capabilities on the red planet.

No matter what the mission, common to all Humvees is a set of hardcore underpinnings: a one and one-quarter-ton truck that sports some of the most rugged off-road capability on the face of the earth.

Along with full-time four-wheel drive, the Humvee has torque-biased Torsen differentials to distribute power to the wheels that can use it best, steep approach and departure angles, 60-percent gradeability and 16 inches of ground clearance as well as a wide stance and low center of gravity, a four-speed automatic transmission for driving ease and soft-soil flotation tires. An independent rear suspension endows the Humvee with good articulation over different kinds of terrain, while radial tires provide its traction. Geared hubs are installed at each wheel to enable AM General to fit smaller brakes.

The original Humvee used a General Motors diesel V-8 engine designed for 15 years or service and to be easy to maintain. Power levels have risen throughout the years, but the Humvee is no speed demon. It can hit 60 mph in less than 20 seconds, but not without a lot of engine noise.

HUMMER

Part troop carrier, part mobile installation, Humvees are multipurpose vehicles even in their most basic forms.

The chassis is all aluminum framing, and the ladder frame is sheathed in riveted aluminum, like some of Jaguar and Land Rover's finer vehicles. The entire vehicle is glued together with Syband, an industrial bonding agent made by American Cyanamid, and held together as the glue cures with 2800 rivets, which in theory could be drilled out afterward, since the Syband forms aerospace-quality bonds.

Early on, AM General had studied using steel to build the Humvee, but the vehicle proved too hefty and too rigid for the kind of duty in its future. Because it's built to flex over some obstacles, when you drive it off-road, it's a squeak, rattle and noise symphony that would make the engineers at Lexus blanch in horror. There is no sound insulation, nor any roll-down windows in the Humvee.

The bodies make no attempt to keep water out. As the Marines found out early on, the vehicle must be able to resist saltwater. After putting the Humvee into service, they reported to AM General that the vehicles' frames were rusting out. The reason? Salt water had been used to rinse them down; in combat scenarios and in training, fresh water is only for cooking and drinking. AM General had to go back in and add about 300 pounds of galvanizing to ensure the reliability of the vehicles. On top of the rustproofing, the Humvee must be able to be turned off in standing water and restart 15 minutes later.

The body is wider than it is tall, with flat sides that make it simpler to judge what alleys and narrow paths it will slide through. The windshield is vertical so it doesn't reflect light in a way that could reveal the vehicle's position. The headlights, too, don't cast light upward for the same reason.

As for camouflage, most Humvees wear a chemical-resistant coating that can repel nerve agents and mustard gas. The coating comes in green camouflage, white and sand camouflage; the Army even specifies the particular pattern for camouflage, no doubt "designed by gnomes at a computer in Langley" according to one AM General executive, and demands it be painted by robots.

Tough road ahead

For AM General, engineering and building the Humvee would be more than a learning experience—it would be a galvanizing lesson in continuous improvement. And it would seem to be lucrative: the initial contract would be worth $1.2 billion. Too, while during the 1970s, in the aftermath of the Vietnam War, the Pentagon's budget had been cut, the Reagan years would bring a budget boom to the Department of Defense—a doubling form $165 billion in 1981 to $330 billion in 1987.

But the numbers clouded the real picture at AM General, which was in turmoil even as it worked earnestly to win the Humvee contract. Its parent company American Motors was in dire financial straits. In 1982, while engineering and development proceeded toward the Humvee project, AMC sold AM General to the LTV Aerospace and Defense Company, where it was set up as the AM General Division of the contractor.

For $170 million, LTV had inherited the company that would win the competition to build what would become the Humvee and the first $1.2 billion contract. Even with the specter of billions of federal dollars coming into its coffers, though, the company's future was in doubt—even before the company's first Humvee was built.

Chapter 3

The Road to Baghdad— and Beyond

We march in precision out of the civilian minivan, penetrating the complex of camo-beige buildings as Air Force-issue HMMWVs cruise by in anonymous grey trim. Outside AM General's manufacturing facility, you'd think we would look patently obvious by driving in something else than a Humvee—but the fleet of Explorers, old Datsuns and middle-aged Cavaliers in the employee parking lot lets us blend right in.

In this day of perimeter checkpoints, invasive body searches and bag matching—just at the daycare center—the ease in getting through security at AM General's manufacturing facility in Mishawaka, Indiana is a little surprising. The main buildings lie just a hundred feet off the surface streets with minimal fencing, and the Sept. 11 effect has had little obvious impact on the workers and guests who enter the AM General campus with a signature and a smile. "We don't sell weapons, we sell trucks," observes AM General spokesman Craig Mac Nab. "We make reinforced anvils."

The war on terror hasn't changed security here that much, he says. That is, until you go inside the factory that builds the Humvee, which, er, hums with activity as we step in line beneath the flags of the 40 different countries and all the U.S. military branches that have been customers of AM General and owners of Humvees. Humvees are in every stage of assembly, some beginning their long military careers as parts in bins, others driving off the assembly line for final checks. One's just been appliquéd with Arabic script near its lift hooks—presumably instructions on operation, not on how to stage a jihad.

Since 1985, AM General has made 165,000 military vehicles for more than 40 countries, from the United States to Djibouti. The U.S. has been, of course, the biggest customer for AM General's vehicles, taking more than 140,000 of the vehicles but the company is not strictly bound to build vehicles for TACOM alone. Depending on the countries, AM General secures permission from the Pentagon to sell to them. The company has the flexibility to build as few or as many vehicles of a kind as the buying nation needs, but the 50 vehicles under construction for the United Arab Emirates are about as small an order as AM General can build at a realistic cost per vehicle (up to $150,000 for specialized versions). But countries as small as Djibouti and Morocco have bought three or four at a time, vehicles close to the specifications from American orders, to keep costs down. That way they can also afford to send soldiers to AM General to learn how to do the preventative maintenance and vehicle checks that the U.S. Army takes care of by itself for its own soldiers. That maintenance—the finer uses of duct tape and hanger wire—as we learn later in the day, can mean life or death for the men and women piloting and riding in Humvees in combat.

Some 50 to 54 different versions of the Humvee, built for specific missions and military applications, fill out the current AM General portfolio. In August of 2003, the company built 57 different versions of the basic Humvee, a record. Twenty to thirty variants is a more typical number, but as the military's mission has become more diverse, the number of Humvee configurations has increased steadily. The longer it serves, the more uses the Pentagon finds for its modern-day war wagon.

Times are good at AM General. In 2003, they built nearly 6,200 vehicles, or about 27 a day. In 2004 they expect to make 6,900 vehicles, including both the military and civilian versions. The production numbers are intentionally kept steady–because unlike the car companies that make vehicles only for consumers, AM General can't build with the hope of selling an extra 10,000 vehicles during a model year through rebates or sales incentives. Humvees trickle out of the plant on a precisely planned schedule not too far ahead of their time, because its main customer is a slow pay.

Imagine if your biggest customer ordered all its products five years in advance–then paid in arrears, sometimes not settling up until the end of the fiscal year. That's the business model of the military contractor, and though AM General was familiar with the system, it hadn't counted on it nearly costing the company its corporate life so soon after it won the contract to build the Humvee.

Money problems

After officially showing the vehicle for the first time at the 1984 Farnborough Air Show in England, AM General began building "Hummers"–a name they quickly licensed for the military HMMWV project they had won, but used here for civilian versions alone–on January 2, 1985.

At that time AM General was confronted with the possibility that, after five years, the Humvee would cease to be. "There was supposed to be a re-buy [a second five-year contract]," says Mac Nab, "but it had been unfunded. So there wasn't going to be a Humvee anymore."

Mac Nab, a veteran of 24 years in the Army, has been AM General's spokesman since 1987. His connections to the Humvee is more than a meal ticket—his oldest daughter served as an Army medic in Germany, driving a Humvee ambulance. Mac Nab revels in the story of AM General and the history of the Humvee, turning tiny facts into legends embroidered by occasional Kipling quotes— entirely appropriate, since he also taught literature for five years at West Point.

Mac Nab had grown up in Rochester, New York, and attended Ithaca College, where he earned a BFA in drama. Drafted a few years out of college, he entered officer training school, then was sent by the Army to graduate school in North Carolina before teaching in the English department at West Point. From West Point, Mac Nab moved to Fort Sill, Okla., then active duty in Korea, and finally Vietnam, where he spent six months as a nuclear weapons employment officer. After his Vietnam tour, Mac Nab landed as a spokesman for the Pentagon, where he worked during much of the time the Humvee was being fielded, and in direct contact with the management of AM General.

Mac Nab also worked in direct contact with the people of the United States, who occasionally enlivened what could be a lonely desk job with a lot of odd phone calls. "You'd never know if it was some lady in Kansas who wanted the CIA to stop irradiating her house so she could take off her tinfoil hat," he recalls.

Or it could be inquiries from infinitesimally small journals like the *Mule News*. Mac Nab recalls a bizarre series of events that led to the belief that the Army had an initiative to use mules in its light infantry divisions, to "train them at the Italian mule school or something. Mules had some utility–though not much, apparently." The story amused him, until a memo announcing a meeting of the mule task force got into the hands of the local UP correspondent, who filed a story based on the reports.

"I got more calls and mail out of that story," a still disbelieving Mac Nab remembers from his file-choked office in downtown South Bend. "Calls from old colonels who worked with mules on the Burma Road. 'You can't use mules anywhere they can't graze – they can't carry their own food and water,' they'd write. One concerned citizen wanted to give me the name and number of the mule expert at the St. Louis Zoo."

"Or could be Walter Pincus from the *New York Times* looking for info on a top-secret nuclear-weapons initiative. Whatever the call was, it was yours–you had to deal with it," he says. "I found I had the right kind of nerves for it. I found it stimulating."

But a long career in the Army had to come to an end. In 1987, "I had just gotten a raise and wouldn't get another for another three years, I wasn't going to come up for colonel for another two or three years–but more to the point, I had kids that were going to be going to college. I couldn't make any more in the Army." On December 1, 1987, Mac Nab was at the Pentagon; on December 2 he reported for duty at AM General.

Mac Nab's long career had prepared him for the trials that he would face as the public relations head for AM General. He understood the arcane system of approving new weapons, getting them into production, educating the press about their uses and victories and failures–and most important, he knew how the relationship between military contractors and the Pentagon often left smaller contractors fighting for additional business in order to survive.

"The government pays for it...but they never pay up front," Mac Nab explains. "We started making trucks in 1984 and delivering in 1985, and then they started paying." But as Mac Nab says, the Pentagon doesn't pay the entire bill—they pay an amount close to the cost, but with enough leeway to ensure they don't overpay contractors for their work. "God forbid the government should ever pay you too much—it's actually against the law," he says. "At the end of the contract, they're gonna make sure they make you whole—but they always make sure [the underpayment] is on the contractor's side."

Too, the contractors like AM General can't operate like conventional automakers like Toyota, which has $26 billion in cash to develop a range of new models before they sell the first one. In addition to being paid in arrears, the contractors can't simply build all the vehicles in a contract at one time and wait to be paid—they must build them at a precise pace that doesn't outstrip the Pentagon's budgets. What the Pentagon and AM General have figured out, Mac Nab says, is how slow they can make the vehicles and still make them at some small pre-ordained profit. "If you make one a year, it'll cost $18 million. If you make three it's not much cheaper. But if you make a hundred...what's the minimum sustaining rate?"

And then there's the issue of competitive bids. The Pentagon must allow new companies to bid on military contracts—regardless of the company's origins or previous experience even though, as Mac Nab points out, "we're making stuff nobody else makes." So long as a company answers a business plan questionnaire, they are qualified to bid on the nation's defense contracts. "That only makes sense if you're going to make something like bullets," he says.

Re-bids can be even more frustrating and bankrupting. Contractors can't assume that, as Mac Nab says, that losing money

The Road to Baghdad—and Beyond

Convoy rules: no one gets left behind.

on the first five-year contract due to start-up costs and engineering will be paid for in the second five-year contract. The contract may not even be renewed. And because the Army is always interested in cutting its costs (one common link with the auto industry) they don't just give the second contract automatically to the company holding the original contract. They own the technical prowess and then they re-bid the contract.

The arduous Humvee development process meant that despite the coming of the Humvee, things were looking grim on AM General's accounting ledgers. The vehicles weren't yet paid for, and what's more, Mac Nab recalls, "it wasn't at all clear that this would be a big winner."

Not only that, the company had essentially put its future in the hands of the Humvee project. In the same year it began building Humvees, AM General had lost a competitive re-bid to build the medium-duty five-ton trucks, a product that had been its core business. AM General also declined to bid on a new contract to make more postal vehicles for the government because of problems with its prototypes, losing the business to Grumman, which had submitted the design for the current wedge-shaped LLVs (long-life vehicles) that deliver the mail.

The result was that, in 1985, "almost everything the company had going was doomed," Mac Nab says. But by the end of 1985, money for Humvees began to appear. AM General was "gradually climbing out of this sea of red," with the caveat that any problems—such as a series of niggling problems in the first year's production—would lead to cost overruns. "If you're going to make any money, it's going to be on the last six months of the contract," he explains, "and if anything goes wrong—if the brake hubs break and you need to weld them on both sides, one of the things that happened—it pushes the [profitability] line down."

The original Humvee contract between the U.S. government and AM General, with options, accounted for 77,000 vehicles, and a total of $1.6 billion due the company. "We made this unbelievable vehicle, to this day an icon for the world," Mac Nab says, "and lost money."

AM General's money problems would be periodic and usually could be traced back to Washington (or more accurately, northern Virginia). Even though the government had begun to pay for the Humvees delivered, the contract ran for only five years, subject to renewal. And in late 1987, upon Mac Nab's arrival in South Bend, it wasn't a sure thing that the Humvee contract would be renewed. The money for the next five-year contract hadn't been put into future budgets.

"This is the sort of thing that I'm not sure that was ever front-page headlines," he says. "We watch the army budget five years out—are they putting money in they need to for our program? Sometimes they don't. Sometimes they forget. Sometimes the money gets shifted around…this year we won't buy Humvees, we'll buy tanks. And in that case, we have to remind them, don't come back next year because we won't be here. You have to buy from us every day, every year, otherwise we'll be gone. You watch that money process, because if you look away for 20 seconds, it'll wander away into someone else's column."

Though it was quickly fixed, the hiccup in future funding came at a sensitive time for AM General. "We were running out. We'd squeezed the last money out of the last Navy contract," Mac Nab says, and the owners at LTV were agitating for AM General to cut costs and boost profits, going so far as to prevent AM General from bidding on another long-term military contract that would have drained LTV's coffers for years before turning in small profits.

"When I came in 1988, it had become clear that the big plant down at Chippewa Avenue, the former Curtis-Wright bomber-engine factory, was underutilized. If we had all the military medium-truck business in the world, the factory would be too big. There were people at LTV that they just wanted to shut that factory down."

At the same time, the Army had begun planning a new range of medium-duty vehicles, including 2 1/2-ton and 5-ton trucks. AM General had begun engineering work and had even sent a representative to Detroit prepared to bid on the business. At some point, the LTV executives decided that the new program was a dead end, and could cost the company $39 million without a guarantee of winning the business. "We sent a guy up to Detroit to bid, but he was called back and not allowed to bid," Mac Nab recalls, "even though it was generally agreed that we would have won – our prototype was better. There was a period of time that the Army was not altogether happy with us because we had a good truck."

AM General's difficult situation with its parent company wouldn't improve, even though the profits did appear after the company won the second five-year contract to build the Humvee. In August of 1989, the Pentagon signed up for an additional 33,331 HMMWVs (options raised the number of vehicles to nearly 50,000 by the end of the term).

Despite the fact that no other company bid for the vehicle, the process brought a new twist to the AM General accounting department. Just because no other company bids for a military contract, "that doesn't mean you automatically get it," Mac Nab says. Instead the Pentagon calls what follows a negotiated sole-source procurement. "What that means is a team of people are going to come and sit on your chest and count the hairs in your nose. They come to your human resources department to tell them the number of pencils they can use.

It took a year to renegotiate the re-buy, Mac Nab says. "We made money on that one. Not an obscene amount of money, though."

Noriega no more

As AM General built them and the military deployed them, the Humvee proved itself to the inner sanctum. "The Humvee has passed all the Army's tests," Mac Nab says. "The soldier test—is the thing in the motor pool, always broken? Does it not carry what it needs to?"

To the public, though, the new military mule was still an unknown. No battle had annealed its image or spread its iconic grille over the airwaves. But a relatively small-scale operation to change the leadership in Panama cast the Humvee as a critical part of the modern military in the eyes of millions of TV viewers who, for the first time, watched America's military actions unfurl in front of the cameras in real time.

In the century of U.S.-Panamanian relations, the country had been mostly a client state of America, from the early 1900s when a U.S.-backed rebellion against Colombia had led to an independent Panama; to the following decade when America cut the canal in Panama that joined the Atlantic and Pacific oceans would be cut; into the late 1970s, when President Jimmy Carter signed a treaty returning the Canal Zone territory to Panama. By the mid-1980s, Panama showed signs of sliding into the kind of military dictatorship that would endanger free trade through the Canal—not to mention might introduce instability even further into Central America, where El Salvador and Nicaragua had already been shattered into chaos. Panamanian presidents since the mid-1980s has mostly been under the control of the country's secret police and its chief, Gen. Manuel Noriega, a former CIA operative indicted on drug-trafficking charges in the U.S. in 1988.

Noriega, known by American intelligence as "the Pineapple" because of his pockmarked face, moved to have Panama's national assembly remove then-president Eric Delvalle in 1988 after Delvalle tried to have him dismissed. Noriega had himself declared "maximum leader" of Panama in December of 1989, and shortly thereafter, declared war against the U.S.

Operation Just Cause began just before Christmas in 1989 to remove the Noriega threat to democracy. On December 20, 27,000 U.S. troops invaded the country after Noriega's forces shot and killed a U.S. Marine stationed in the nation's capital. American and Panamanian forces clashed while Noriega himself took refuge in the Vatican Embassy. And in infamous scenes played before viewing audiences on the Cable News Network (CNN) and broadcast news, U.S. forces attempted to dislodge Noriega by playing rock music 24 hours a day, giving Noriega and his defenders little peace.

In short order, U.S. forces took control of Panama and by January 3, Noriega had surrendered. The action had given CNN a huge ratings boost—indeed, in less than a decade on the air, CNN had become the nation's on-air news source, so ubiquitous in its coverage that media critics coined a new phrase, "CNN syndrome"—meaning that in times of national events, viewers turned in droves to the channel, only to leave when the action was over. So universal had CNN become, in the U.S. and around the world, that when the U.S. invaded Panama, the Soviet Union's foreign ministry didn't call the U.S. embassy to condemn the action—it sent a statement to CNN's Moscow bureau where it could be aired to maximum effect.

The Panama action and the CNN effect gave the Humvee its chance in the spotlight. Mac Nab remembers the action and the response from retired Army colleagues who were watching the new Humvees emerge from Army motor pools into the country's consciousness. 'How did you manage to get a picture of the Humvee in every scrap of footage from Panama and the Middle East?' they would ask," Mac Nab says.

It was also the beginning of the Humvee legend of saving the lives of soldiers. Mac Nab and AM General began to get stories from the front of Humvee heroics: one Humvee dropped into Panama by parachute landed upside down in a mud pit, was rolled over and driven right off into combat. One soldier reported to AM General that the windshield in his Humvee took a bullet for him—a bullet that starred the windshield right in front of his face.

The action had cost the U.S. 23 lives, while hundreds of Panamanian soldiers and civilians were killed. Flown to the U.S. and later convicted on drug and money laundering charges, Noriega is eligible for parole in 2006.

Desert Storm gathers

Just nine months after Noriega's capture, another tinhorn dictator with much more vicious tendencies would move from the sidelines to the center of the geopolitical scene. His inhuman urges not sated from eight years of war with neighboring Iran, or from killing thousands of Kurdish citizens in their own country, Iraq's Saddam Hussein would, by the summer of 1990, give a coalition of U.S. and international soldiers reason to attack him in the Middle East under a united force.

Saddam Hussein's gamble in invading neighboring Kuwait would cast him as the chief agitant among a slew of problematic Middle Eastern leaders. He would become a pillar of anti-terrorist policy, later a detainee charged with war crimes, and for more than a decade a kind of political bogeyman: a serious threat to those involved in the military and intelligence realms, a punchline to others, even earning a spot as the domineering, sex-crazed spouse of

Satan in the hilariously vulgar animated film *South Park: Bigger, Longer and Uncut.*

Hussein would also, indirectly, give the Humvee its biggest lift in becoming the world-conquering brand it is today. Whether charging across the desert in a *Dr. Zhivago* homage or patrolling a liberated Kuwait City, Hussein cast the Humvee's image as the critical sidekick to soldiers and Abrams tank, Apache helicopters, aircraft carriers and cargo planes alike.

As Mac Nab believes, "It was really the Operation Desert Shield building where everyone saw them and said, Martha, what are those things?"

The threat to humanity from Saddam Hussein had many nuances. He was a killer: from 1980 to 1988 he confronted neighboring Iran in a war in which atrocities were the battlefield norm. Hussein used chemical weapons against Iranian soldiers in that time, and turned those weapons on Iraqi citizens in 1988 as well, killing an estimated 5,000 Kurds in the northern Iraqi city of Halabja. Hussein also had interest in developing weapons that could be used against more remote targets, including Israel.

Hussein killed and encouraged others in his Ba'ath Party elite to do the same. His sons Uday and Qusay held positions in the Iraqi government and used their power in hellish ways. Uday controlled the Iraqi media as well as the country's Olympic team, members of which were reportedly tortured for poor athletic performances, while Qusay eventually became a member of the Ba'ath Party's ruling committee.

Hussein's motives for invading neighboring Kuwait in 1990 were clear: the oil-rich nation was friendly with the United States, and had better oil fields than the California-sized Iraq. By Hussein's rationale, Kuwait had always been Iraq's nineteenth province and should be reunited with the rest of the country, obliterating nearly a

The Road to Baghdad—and Beyond

The Humvee drops in: military spec allows them to be "unloaded" from 15 feet off the ground at 200 mph air speed.

century of adherence to the haphazardly drawn borders of the Middle East concocted in the aftermath of World War I.

Just months after U.S. forces had dislodged Noriega from Panama, Iraqi forces invaded Kuwait. On August 2, 1990, Iraq soldiers poured into the lightly defended and, with more than 25 percent of the world's known reserves, oil-rich nation, even richer than Iraq in that respect. Iraq's public stance was that it was invading to allow Kuwaitis to choose their own leadership: Iraq's ambassador to the United States, Mohammed al-Mashat, told the Bush administration that "Iraqi forces will be withdrawn as soon as the situation has settled down, and as soon as the free government of Kuwait has so wished. We hope that this will be a matter of a few days, or a few weeks at the latest."

Iraq never would withdraw—it would have to be expelled. And in the course of the remainder of 1990, Iraq began to commit the kind of atrocities in Kuwait that had occurred in Iran. Kuwait's Sheik Jaber al-Ahmed al-Sabah, had escaped into neighboring Saudi Arabia in his Mercedes, but Kuwaitis left behind were imprisoned and tortured; many simply disappeared. The nation's museums were sacked, public buildings were destroyed.

Worse, for the world community, Iraq had destroyed a delicate sense of balance that had held the region in vague stability. There was no peace to have broken, what with the Israeli-Palestinian issue simmering, Syria engaged in Lebanon and Iran under the control of militant fundamentalists. But Iraq had upset the rough truces holding the region's powers away from each others' throats.

Kuwait pleaded for U.S. help; the Saudis looked to America to make sure they weren't the next to be invaded. And while the Russian and Chinese governments called for Iraq to back down, it was President George H.W. Bush from the U.S. and Great Britain's Margaret Thatcher that took the issue to the United Nations to seek permission for military action. "The economic aspects of this are well-known to the American people," Bush concluded. "And long run economic effects on the free world could be devastating."

Bush and new British Prime Minister John Major took the case to the United Nations Security Council late in 1990. The Council passed a resolution demanding Iraq withdraw from the territory by January 15, 1991, and authorized the use of force if it did not. The threat of the world's fourth-largest army with SCUD missiles capable of penetrating to Israel had become a reality, though: Hussein had begun lobbing missiles in the direction of forces gathering to protect Israel and Saudi Arabia and retake Kuwait. What had been known as Operation Desert Shield would become Operation Desert Storm when Hussein failed to respond to the U.N.'s call.

On Jan. 17, 1991, thunderclaps and sonic booms lit the sky over Baghdad as American and British air forces began bombing the Iraqi capital. For a month, air strikes softened up the Iraqi's defenses, producing a nightly news show filled with fireworks and terrific blasts, decimated chunks of Baghdad. Then on Feb. 23, hours after a deadline President Bush had given for Hussein to leave Kuwait had expired, a coalition of U.S. and British forces penetrated into Kuwait by land and sea.

Within hours of the invasion of Kuwait, coalition forces would be into Iraqi territory in what military officials called the largest invasion since World War II. An armada of Blackhawk and Chinook helicopters from the 101st Airborne took to the skies, dropping 50 Humvees into the war zone for use as part of the ground assault.

The Humvee would become the workhorse of Operation Desert Storm. The presence of CNN in Baghdad and throughout the staging area for the war gave the Humvee an instant audience in the hundreds of millions, as America tuned into what would be the most comprehensively televised war ever fought to its time. Humvees were in action transporting troops, dodging land mines, and launching TOW missiles into the Iraqis' defenses. The sand-colored "new Jeep" seemed to be all over the television screen, playing to a much wider audience than in the mission to dethrone Noriega.

But it wasn't merely a "new Jeep." The Humvee's multiple missions gave it a tougher edge in combat—an all-around capability that the Jeep never had been designed for. The Humvee translated immediately and durably into a new metaphor for the U.S. military. The workhorse of the Gulf War would be a stovetop for MREs (Meals Ready to Eat) as soldiers cooked on its manifold. A bed, where soldiers would sleep on its hood for brief naps that substituted for real sleep. A place to eat. A modern-day cavalry where the hood of the Humvee become a tactical planning meeting. The side mirrors worked for shaving on the offhand chance a soldier got to shower and clean up. But at the same time, the Humvee was a hard-charging, seriously capable war tool that could carry .50-caliber machine guns and TOW missiles, grenade launchers and Stinger missiles even while, as *Forbes* recalls, one Humvee would serve in a Catholic mass as an altar where a chalice of sacramental wine was placed in one of the first services held after the cease-fire was announced.

Lt. Col. Bill Weber, a U.S. Army observer-controller, had first-hand experience with the Humvee's versatility. "I'd go over nine-inch logs easily, I'd go over ditches easily, muddy terrain, rocky terrain, it didn't matter as long as you used good judgment," he said. "Trust me, it would go places a jeep wouldn't even think about."

The tales from the Persian Gulf War were frightening and awesome enough to read, much less to see firsthand. Showcased in footage from the war as a military machine and a lethal weapon, the Humvee burned itself into war memories like those of Gunnery Sgt. Angel Estrala, of Tucson, Ariz., who told the Associated Press about the night his Humvee charged into the Kuwaiti desert on the first night of the Gulf War, crossing an anti-tank mine and getting blown in the air:

"There was a big blast, the vehicle picks up into the air and I saw the tire flying through the air, then we hit the ground," Estrala said. *"We had sandbags on the floorboard, so I survived."*

The explosion blew the front end from the vehicle, but the five Marines inside survived only to encounter Iraqi artillery fire. Estrala left the wreckage of his own Humvee, the wire reported, and took over his squad leader's Humvee to keep the battle in sight.

Operation Desert Storm lasted only a few weeks, and in its opening hours it had become clear that the threat of the world's fourth-largest army was less convincing in reality than in prewar intelligence. Allied troops took more than 10,000 prisoners as they dodged through Kuwaiti territory and the hundreds of fires set to oil fields by the retreating Iraqi army. About 200,000 coalition troops took to the charge, encountering little resistance as they swept Hussein's military out of Kuwait and pressed deep into Iraq. As Cpl. Mark Thieme, a Humvee TOW gunner from suburban Washington, D.C., told the *Washington Post,* his unit moved so quickly in the dark they had no clue how deep in Iraqi territory they were.

By Feb. 26, 1991, Allied troops had taken control of Kuwait. And two days later, Pres. Bush announced a cease-fire, leaving Hussein in power within his own country. The declared objective of the war had been accomplished—though afterward, Hussein would reassert his authority, where the U.S. had hoped a popular uprising would topple him from power. More than 600 Kuwaitis were missing and presumed dead in the action; more than a thousand Kuwaitis were confirmed dead and 20,000 had been detained in jails or sent to Iraq, where many were tortured during the seven months of the occupation. Among U.S. forces, some 293 were killed, with 148 of those in combat and 145 in accidents.

Like other weapons systems the Humvee had emerged as a technologically advanced, superior weapon developed for a military that only 20 years before had been seen in decline. Vietnam had worn down the nation's opinion of its military and with the accession of Ronald Reagan in 1980, and a revival had been long due. Vast increases in military spending and improvements in recruiting, morale and training had worked: by the time of the Gulf War the army had undergone a cultural and technical revolution that catapulted U.S. forces to the front ranks of the world's military. "There's no question, this is the best Army any of us has ever seen," retired Gen. William R. Richardson, former commander of the Army's Training and Doctrine Command and one of the architects of the Army's renewal, told the *Los Angeles Times*.

The Humvee also had the benefit of becoming a recurring character on the nation's most-watched TV show of its day–the Gulf War. CNN's coverage of the war–reporters like Peter Arnett were calling in from Baghdad hotels in the middle of bombing–had boosted the network's ratings to unseen levels, more than from 27 percent to tenfold, depending on which numbers were to be believed. The Gulf War had changed American media: now, in the words of CNN anchor Wolf Blitzer, America watched what was happening instead of reading about it the next morning.

The Gulf War was over–sort of. With Hussein still in power but turned out of Kuwait, the U.S.-led mission was turned over to the United Nations to enforce resolutions that Iraq destroy all its weapons of mass destruction, including nuclear, chemical and biological weapons, as well as missiles with a range of more than 93 miles. The resolution set up a U.N. inspections commission to oversee the process. President Bush, riding a wave of public opinion over the apparent success of the war, used the occasion to outline a policy that would change the Middle East for the better, a "new world order," he outlined in his address to America:

> Tonight I come to this House to speak about the world – the world after war.
>
> The recent challenge could not have been clearer. Saddam Hussein was the villain, Kuwait the victim. To the aid of this small country came nations from North America and Europe, from Asia and South America, from Africa and the Arab world, all united against aggression.
>
> Our uncommon coalition must now work in common purpose to forge a future that should never again be held hostage to the darker side of human nature.
>
> Tonight in Iraq, Saddam walks amidst ruin. His war machine is crushed. His ability to threaten mass destruction is itself destroyed. His people have been lied to, denied the truth. And when his defeated legions come home, all Iraqis will see and feel the havoc he has wrought. And this I promise you: for all that Saddam has done to his own people, to the Kuwaitis, and to the entire world, Saddam and those around him are accountable.
>
> Now, we can see a new world coming into view. A world in which there is the very real

prospect of a new world order. In the words of Winston Churchill, a "world order" in which "the principles of justice and fair play ... protect the weak against the strong..." A world where the United Nations, freed from cold war stalemate, is poised to fulfil the historic vision of its founders. A world in which freedom and respect for human rights find a home among all nations.

The Gulf war put this new world to its first test, and, my fellow Americans, we passed that test.

The Hummer Mystique

The ramifications of the lightning war in Iraq in 1991 still reverberate today. War with Iraq gave George H.W. Bush a presidential legacy the reverse of his image to that date. It steeled his policy and sent his popularity soaring. But a post-war recession took it all away just as swiftly as the coalition had booted Hussein from Kuwait. Bush lost the 1992 presidential election—in AM General-speak, the presidential re-buy of 1992 didn't materialize. A relative unknown in national politics, William Jefferson Clinton, won the November election and would take office even though the recession that had cost Bush re-election had already begun to abate.

The Iraq war also gave AM General's pride and joy a national audience. AM General had made the typical moves to publicize its vehicle to its military audiences. "LTV was pretty good at [that]," Mac Nab recalls, including publicizing the Humvee in the Marine Corps gazette in the early 1990s. LTV had taken the vehicle on media tours and road shows and had placed stories in military newspapers about how great the new war wagon was. But nothing could compare to the endorsement of the U.S. military, 24 hours a

The Road to Baghdad—and Beyond

Humvees are designed with special hooks, used to transport them by helicopter into action.

day, seven days a week, broadcast live from halfway around the globe. The Humvee was a real American success story—and Saddam Hussein had helped make it so.

The Humvee had touched a deep vein of American pride, battered by Vietnam. Here was a sort of national treasure—a vehicle that had proved American mettle in its sheetmetal, a vehicle on which it would be redundant to put an American flag. For sure, every American watching CNN for war coverage knew what a Humvee was and what it meant—as did the Kuwaitis awaiting their liberators and the Iraqis alike.

That the Humvee was almost purely American didn't hurt its credentials. Assembled in the Rust Belt, on a low-tech assembly line by workers wearing Ball State sweatshirts from 97-percent U.S.-sourced pieces (the frame rails come from Venezuela; the geared hubs, from Mexico), the Humvee was and is built with union labor by the United Auto Workers Local #5.

"We have a product that's true Americana," says Mac Nab. "And it's better than anything anyone else makes...Germans...Japs...and people know that."

Unpredictably, the war coverage had provided the fuel it needed to take its Humvee in an entirely new direction—into the garages of wealthy toy collectors first, and suburbanites later. AM General started hearing from civilians. While the company couldn't actually sell the vehicles—they were built on government contract, after all—civilians were writing in by the dozen, asking if the Humvee could be purchased. "I've received letters from folks all over the country who want one," Mac Nab told the AP in early 1992.

But one special owner would spearhead the movement to allow Humvees to be sold to the public. He brought his own hardcore action credentials to the table when he pushed AM General's execs to start making Humvees for civilians shortly after the first war with Iraq ended.

"We made an exception for Arnie," a spokesman told *BusinessWeek*, referring to Arnold Schwarzenegger. "But he only wants to drive his to Spago."

Chapter 4

The Terminator and the Hummer

The Humvee charged across the deserts of Iraq and promptly etched its silhouette into America's iconography. Like other overnight superstars, years of hard work had preceded its meteoric rise. And like other superstars, the Humvee launched itself from the bit-player ranks into household recognition across the country in the ultimate reality TV show, only to become basically unattainable.

Surely Saddam Hussein had kicked off the Humvee's first wave of publicity through a bluff. But it would be Arnold Schwarzenegger who would flatten Benzes, Lexuses and Ferraris into also-rans with the civilian Hummer, making it the most coveted Hollywood accessory since the Oscar.

And in a switch from the Hollywood norm, the relationship between Schwarzenegger and the Hummer sprang from the star's own enthusiasm, not from a multi-million-dollar marriage of convenience. Celebrity endorsements are the stock and trade of lesser-paid actors: Halle Berry's Academy Award doesn't get as much screen time as her makeup commercials, and stars like Bruce Willis regularly tap into foreign markets—Japan, in his case—to film ads that bankroll their lifestyles while not intruding too much on their American audience's sensibilities. Arnold and his Hummer share something deeper. A true fan of military vehicles, Arnold didn't just leap onto the bandwagon alone, he drove it—and has been with AM General for more than a decade, though surely he has had lust in his heart for other brands.

His contribution to the Humvee's iconography can't easily be traced through to AM General's bottom line. But, then again, how many brands can say their celebrity pitchman's mission in another life was "to crush my enemies and hear the lamentation of their women?" Without Schwarzenegger's lust for the Humvee, it's arguable that AM General might never have been able to certify the Humvee for public use as the civilian Hummer, or that it would have been able to sell enough to the public to justify a decade of sales without the Terminator's celebrity intertwined with its own.

The Humvee vaulted into the nation's living room while Arnold staggered across its movie screens, mouthing stiff one-liners and grooming himself to become a Hollywood titan. They met by chance—and from then on, neither one of them would ever be the same.

Living in America

There is no shrewder Hollywood businessman than Arnold Schwarzenegger, nor one more keenly attuned to merchandising his own image. By chance or luck, both he and the Humvee were defining their careers in the same span of time—and when they came together, it played out like a buddy picture with perfect casting.

Schwarzenegger's story began in Austria. Born July 30, 1947 in Austria, Schwarzenegger grew up not far from where the Mercedes-Benz Gelaendewagen, a sort of German Humvee or Land Rover, is built. The quintessential self-made American didn't actually come to America until the age of 21 on a B-1 visa, which allows athletes to visit America to compete and train, but prevents them from earning money from American companies. Schwarzenegger says in his 1977 autobiography that he had worked out an agreement with Joe Weider, publisher of several fitness magazines including *Flex*, *Muscle & Fitness* and *Men's Fitness* to be paid for pictures and writing while he was on his initial visa. At least one California newspaper has suggested that this may have violated Schwarzenegger's visa conditions, but nonetheless in November 1969 he received an H-2 visa allowing him to work in the U.S. In 1974 he became a permanent resident of the U.S. and took his oath of citizenship in 1983. While under Weider's wing Schwarzenegger participated in the movie that would give him his first hint of celebrity, the weightlifting documentary *Pumping Iron*. Not truly an acting role, the film gave Schwarzenegger a taste of Hollywood that he would parlay into a string of typecast bit parts, like playing Jayne Mansfield's bodybuilding husband Mickey Hargitay in 1980's *Jayne Mansfield Story*.

But it was another goal that seems to have teamed. While he acted, he also finished coursework for a bachelor of arts degree at the University of Wisconsin-Superior, majoring in business administration and marketing. The rare actor with a higher education, Schwarzenegger proceeded to turn his budding stardom into something far larger and lucrative.

Schwarzenegger's first true hit was 1982's *Conan the Barbarian*, a laughably entertaining comic-book adventure flick. As Conan, Arnold learned the true power of celluloid: the ability to

HUMMER

Arnold Schwarzenegger receives one of the first H2s for his birthday.

deliver nonsensical lines that somehow lived on in the minds of his fans despite the incongruously thick Austrian accent. "What is best in life? To crush your enemies, to see them driven before you, and to hear the lamentations of their women."

By wisely choosing populist and science-action scripts over the rest of the decade, Schwarzenegger became the single most identifiable voice on the silver screen, even with the accent. "I'll be back," he intoned in his most successful film, *The Terminator*, which cemented his status as Hollywood's action-movie king and took in $38 million at the box office, a strong performance for 1984. Throwaways like *Red Sonja* and *Conan the Destroyer* reinforced the notion, though, that "Ah-nuld" was a one-note act.

Wisely, Arnold moved his career out of the action arena in 1988 with *Twins* where his willingness to be the brunt of his own jokes endeared him in an otherwise slack script. Humor worked better in his next action outing, *Total Recall*, which blended a witty script with pure visual thrill and one of Sharon Stone's more memorable screen roles in which she is both naked with Arnold and killed by him within a span of few minutes.

Never in danger of receiving an acting award himself, Arnold spent the decade bankrolling non-acting business endeavors and investments in companies like Microsoft and Starbucks that boosted his personal wealth far above $500 million (today, some estimates place it as high as $800 million). Savvy financial moves enabled a lifestyle that even in Hollywood could be seen as extravagant: Arnold is said to prefer $3,000 Giacomo suits and custom-made $36,000 Audemars Piguet watches. "Sometimes Arnold sees people or some of his friends wearing other watches," president of Audemars Piguet's North American division Francois-Henry Bennahmias told music television network VH1, "and he'll come up to them and say, 'That's a girlie watch.'"

Physical displays of wealth aren't limited to his body, although the Terminator is said to love pedicures. Arnold's holdings include a $4.5 million yacht with a state-of-the-art entertainment center; a compound in Brentwood; a ski lodge in Sun Valley; a Boeing 747 he leases to Singapore Airlines; original artwork by Marc Chagall and Norman Rockwell; and a restaurant, Schatzi (German for "sweetheart") in Santa Monica, Calif.

In his films, Arnold favored high-tech machinery, explosive rides and Armageddon-quality explosions. Off screen, he was known to like his action toys loud, fast, and unattainable by mere mortals, too. His riches also include a collection of vehicles with a pronounced militaristic streak. Schwarzenegger tracked down and now owns the M47 tank he drove as a member of the Austrian military in the 1960s. The tank had been buried during the Cold War, with just the turret poking above ground, then dug up and shipped to the Motts Military Museum in Groveport, Ohio, which keeps it on display for Schwarzenegger. Museum operator Warren Motts told the Associated Press that, "One lawyer told me, 'He's not nearly as interested in a $40 million movie deal as he is in what happens to this tank.'" Schwarzenegger also owns a custom-made Pinzgauer, a six-wheel off-roader that has been manufactured in Austria.

But his collection wouldn't be complete without one more military vehicle he spotted while filming in Oregon in 1990. As the legend tells it, his fascination with the Humvee led to the development of a version that AM General could sell to the public. The problem was, it didn't exist yet in civilian form. But could any company, never mind the U.S. military, deny a man who owned his own tank?

Getting down to civvies

Long before the stars came calling on Indiana, AM General could see that the post-Iraq landscape was changing. "As long as there's an armed forces, there's going to be a need for vehicles...but the defense industry is changing, and we need to diversify," spokesperson Susan Carney told the *Los Angeles Times* in 1992.

AM General hardly saw the wholesale adoption of the Humvee by Hollywood coming. President Jim Armour told auto journalist Matt DeLorenzo that, "to me, it always seemed obvious that if the Humvee as the latest technology, the best 4x4 in the world, and designed to be the modern replacement for the Jeep, it would eventually go into the commercial arena." The company had been busied with truck programs and its survival in the 1980s and that had delayed working on a civilian version of the Humvee, but Armour says that work began in 1988 on converting the war wagon into a consumer vehicle.

Even then, AM General believed the potential for the civilian Hummer would lie in extreme off-road uses, perfect for utility companies, farmers and ranchers, search and rescue teams, even exploration and oil drilling companies—a duty the Chinese government has assigned to a few Humvees it purchased in the 1990s.

They didn't know they would also be appealing to one of the top box-office draws of all time. In 1990, on the set of *Kindergarten Cop*, a mild action-comedy hit for Paramount, Schwarzenegger saw a Humvee troop carrier wind by. Soon after, he told AM General executives, he read an article in *Motor Trend* magazine in which the magazine took part in a 55-day rally from London to Beijing behind the wheel of civilian prototype Hummers. Enchanted by the look of the vehicle ("I needed a vehicle that matched the expressiveness of my personality") Schwarzenegger began to inquire through a third party if the Hummer was yet for sale.

The problem was, although work had begun on the civilian Hummer, the company hadn't decided yet whether it would be a worthwhile project. "'We don't make it yet,' we told him," says

AM General's Mac Nab, "but we decided, let's poke at this and make a way."

Within a year, Arnold had become the first non-military customer for the Humvee, or Hummer. Over the summer of 1991, after winning permission for non-com sales from the Pentagon, AM General had converted Arnold's Humvee to meet relevant safety standards, then installed an interior in a shop in Michigan. Arnold, apparently, had to be dissuaded from a vehicle equipped with its own gun turret: "We convinced him that a turret would leak down his neck." He also was forbidden to order a camouflaged vehicle because, as Mac Nab, suggests, "The lawyers wouldn't like that." After a few visits back and forth, Schwarzenegger's vehicle had been completed and signed by the workers at the AM General plant. It would be the first of a number of Hummers he would own, including some with a custom-fitted bar and television in the back, one with a red decal signifying the Austrian city of Graz, and one with a custom interior that seats he, his wife Maria Shriver and their three children more comfortably.

Shortly before delivering Schwarzenegger's vehicle–and near the summer debut of his latest action film *Terminator 2*–AM General announced in June 1991 that it would sell the Hummer to the public. A year later in October of 1992, AM General sold its first civilian Hummer. Five models were offered: two- and four-seat hardtops, a four-seat model with a canvas top, a two-seat hardtop for fleet use, and a four-door, four-seat wagon. The original Hummer for civilians shared the body and powertrains (a 150-hp, 6.2-liter V-8 diesel). The engine came from General Motors, as did the three-speed automatic transmission. A central tire inflation system allowed drivers to change tire pressures without having to leave the cockpit–something not even the military versions offered. Tan, black, red and white paint were offered, as well as military green or camouflage CARC paint. The base price was $46,550.

The vehicle came to market with Arnold's implicit endorsement, from *Road & Track* magazine's review of the new Hummer: "When I drove it for the first time, that's when it became a whole new world. It was not just now so visually interesting for me, but it was perfect when you drive it because the more bumpy the roads got, the smoother the ride got. It doesn't just look ballsy, but it's really rugged in what it can handle. To me that's the ultimate in a vehicle."

The Hummer meshed perfectly with Arnold's public persona—perhaps after careful consideration, according to one of his acquaintances. "He uses his props rather well," George Butler, *Pumping Iron*'s filmmaker. "Arnold learned very early that in America, particularly the America of the '70s and '80s...there was a new era and it was about strength, health, wealth, narcissism and power. Arnold got that."

Car's the star

It's clear that the star power of Arnold Schwarzenegger benefited the Hummer in a way no other vehicle nor its patrons can claim. Rallyist Erik Carlsson is an ambassador for Saab, as comedian Jerry Seinfeld is for Porsche and *Tonight Show* host Jay Leno is for classic cars in general. Arnold's attachment to Hummer is the one relationship that didn't come long after the vehicle in question already was well established in the marketplace—in addition to being the first sport-utility vehicle to draw that kind of star power.

The Hummer's relative lack of power and speed nonetheless has drawn celebrities of every stripe. Among the people who have owned or driven Hummers are racers Al Unser Sr. and Jr.; tennis ace Andre Agassi; career pixie Bjork; lionesque actor Lorenzo Lamas, hoops legend Dr. J (Julius Irving), Erik Estrada, Fabio, Coolio, Dennis Rodman, Howard Stern, James Earl Jones (the voice of CNN), Roseanne, Ted Turner, Tom Clancy, and Don King, Gary Coleman, porn queen Jenna Jameson, George Foreman, Mike Tyson and Montel Williams. Long before the Cadillac Escalade emerged on the hip-hop scene, the Hummer was the favorite video companion to Tupac Shakur, whose 1996 Hummer was sold on eBay after his death; Hummers also have appeared in videos by 50 Cent, Missy Elliott, Tupac, Puff Daddy and the Notorious B.I.G.

The Hummer's movie appearances range from box office smashes like *A Few Good Men (1992), Last Action Hero (1993), Clear and Present Danger (1994), Crimson Tide (1995), Independence Day (1996), The Lost World (1997)* to *Blackhawk Down (2002)*. Arnold himself wasn't able to work the Hummer into a movie of his own until 1994's *Last Action Hero*, in which he appears with wife Shriver idling up to a movie premiere in his Hummer.

That kind of guerrilla marketing had never been attempted with a vehicle capable of guerilla warfare. With Arnold, AM General didn't need the transcendentalism of modern "emotional marketing" – in one fell swoop the Hummer already had the grassroots support it needed to transform the Humvee from a vehicle that high school grads drove into danger in swamps into a sort of G.I. Joe action piece that buffed celebs' images – or at least drew attention to them. Because of his name it had become an object so unintentionally luxurious, Neiman Marcus offered his and hers Hummers in its 1991 holiday catalog.

Humvee to Hummer

Even with celebrities pulling up to the red carpet in Hummers, the trendy statement still didn't make much sense. Why does anyone need anything this big, this raw, this unrefined? The short answer is they don't. Hummer enthusiasts then and now are of the most extreme stripe, in a rarified strata of income and achievement that enables them to buy a life-sized toy an transform themselves into action heroes.

Transforming the Humvee itself into a civilian product took long hours and lots of head scratching. How to deal with leaks? The Humvee hadn't been built leakproof—in fact the military wanted water to be able to drain in and out of the body. Paying customers wouldn't tolerate window frames dribbling on their Armani suits. How to retrofit a sound system in a vehicle that clattered and creaked enough to drown out a Metallica CD? What about sound deadening? And was there a way to add power to a package that couldn't even out-accelerate a $10,000 Geo Metro three-cylinder hatchback?

Indeed there are myriad differences between the Hummer and the Humvee. While the Humvee is the Hummer's DNA—it doesn't work without it—the Hummer has significant changes to make it suitable for on-road driving.

Most of the Humvee's original equipment carries over into civilian versions. The Hummer, like the Humvee, is capable of negotiating 30 inches of water, climbing 22 inch ledges, and scaling extreme 60 percent inclines, declines and 40 percent side slopes, and can cover on- or off-road trails in severe weather all while carrying a full payload of 12,100 pounds. The body, driveline, venting, four-speed automatic, four-wheel-drive system, and frame are very similar or identical to military versions.

In changing the Humvee into the Hummer, AM General made a raft of modifications. They had to seal it up and install drain plugs. Instead of polycarbonate fragment protection—"transparent armor"—in the window areas, the Hummer came equipped with glass windows and windshields. And instead of a gun turret, Hummer buyers received an altogether more pedestrian dome light. As the decade progressed, AM General would add power locks,

HUMMER

GM's interpretation of the HUMMER design is spot-on, from the narrow grille to the exposed suspension.

windows and mirrors; better sound systems; and in 1995, a gasoline engine, a GM 5.7-liter V-8 with 190 hp, to the Hummer's list of creature comforts. Also added to the list were ever-increasing dollars in the price tag. By the end of the decade a base Hummer topped the $65,000 mark.

Still, even with the more car-like features bolted on its military frame, it's difficult to imagine a less pleasing vehicle to drive on public roads. The Hummer's edges are barely softened in translation. It's essential to love its essence before consigning yourself to drive one on the streets.

The Hummer's size is chief among its drawbacks. Though the hood is squared off and the sides are vertical, leaving no mystery as to the vehicle's dimensions, it can be a challenge just to find places to park the beast, and patience is always a requirement for multi-point maneuvers. Driving in narrowed lanes on the Interstate is even spookier; you're forever in fear of drifting into the family Camry in the next lane. The ride is often harsh; the huge tires thud over bumps, though taking them at speed softens them more than navigating them carefully.

Inside, the Hummer offers remarkably little in the way of room and comfort, separated its passengers by a three-foot-wide expanse of drivetrain tunnel. It's almost impossible to have a normal conversation with the noise and the distance.

Time is of the essence, too, when driving a Hummer. Acceleration is leisurely and passing times are best left in theory. It's a long, slow drag to get to highway speeds and once you're there, applying the brakes to slow down the whole affair seems counterproductive. The diesel engine isn't one of the nicer ones on the road, either; it clatters like the Dubuque road production of *Stomp!* The engine noise is complemented by roaring tire noise, the occasional suspension and body noises, and omnipresent wind noise —in the words of one journalist, a fearsome din that sounds like "Dorothy's house on the way to Oz."

None of those flaws mean much, though, when the first stranger recognizes the Hummer first and thinks they know who you are. "You're a hockey guy, right?" In one 500-mile drive, that was the least expected answer, lumped in along with football player, NASCAR driver and car-company employee.

Before Arnold, any rational onlooker would have believed a Hummer driver would be an off-duty soldier. But soon enough, being seen in a Hummer in the Hollywood Hills became a sign that you had arrived. Hummers showed up in car-rental fleets and limousine liveries. And though some women caught on to the craze, it was largely a man thing, all puns intended: nearly 80 percent of Hummer drivers in the early years were men aged 40-45 with an average income of $150,000 or more per year.

Its pitfalls didn't matter to the exclusive few who could own and drive them. And it was that high-dollar, high-octane set of consumers that drew the interest of America's biggest carmaker in 1999 as it looked for a way to draw some glitter back to its famous but tarnished brand.

But first, the Hummer had to grow. Its reputation had been forged in war, but now it was time for some charity work to burnish its reputation in an idealized, Norman Rockwell way. The Hummer would head around the globe as a tool in a shifting U.S. military mission that, more often than not in the intervening decade, would be for peace rather than war.

Chapter 5

War and Peace

Bill Clinton's presidential victory in 1992 ushered in a new era of prosperity for America—and wilting budgets for the American military. The former governor of Arkansas slid to victory with less than a majority in the popular vote, thanks to the third-party candidacy of H. Ross Perot that drew conservative voters away from President George H.W. Bush. Bush's electoral problems were clearly defined: purposeful in Iraq but not a victor, unresponsive to an economy that refused to turn out of recession until it was too late, and lacking in telegenic appeal, an essential quality in a televised age. In contrast, Clinton, a brilliant and natural politician, was young, handsome and benefited from a third-tier political career that gave him a blank slate to sell to the electorate. Style won out over substance, and the quintessential feel-good president would take office just as the economy, Bush's electoral albatross, had begun to take flight.

Clinton would preside over an unprecedented economic expansion during his two terms as president—some of it seeded during the prior administration, but mostly due to Clinton's fortitude in resolving the budget deficits that had accumulated during the Reagan/Bush years. But his antagonistic relationship with the U.S. military would undercut his legacy, from poorly timed "Don't ask, don't tell" policies to the devaluation of the military from defensive force to international peacekeepers. But his most troubling legacy with the nation's military would come at the budget table. Untouched by the Vietnam draft and unseasoned by military experience on the federal or personal level, Clinton slashed the nation's defense budget, leaving black ink on the ledgers and gaping black holes in the Pentagon's funding.

During the Clinton decade the Pentagon had to simultaneously meet objectives to modernize the military on slack budgets and provide its forces to nations emerging from civil war—all on less money, save for an election-year boost of the defense budget by nearly 7 percent in fiscal year 2001. "Since 1992, when President Clinton took office, our armed forces have deployed an average of one deployment every nine weeks, yet defense budgets have declined by nearly 40 percent during that same time, and procurement of modern weapons systems has declined by 70 percent," noted Senator John McCain, R-Ariz.

Clinton reduced spending significantly during his two terms, from an estimated 22.5 percent of the gross domestic product (GDP) in 1992 to 20 percent. But as the nonprofit, nonpartisan National Center of Policy Analysis (NCPA) noted, three-quarters of the spending drop came directly from lower defense spending, which fell from 4.9 percent of the GDP in 1992 to 3.1 percent. Clinton, the think tank thinks, had balanced the budget at the expense of the nation's defense.

Budget cuts would reduce defense spending to a percent of the GDP not seen since the Great Depression—and the Republican opposition agreed that America was no longer in need of a Cold War-sized defense budget. However, the U.S. Senate Republican Policy Committee issued a statement in 1998 that declared Clinton's policies had put the military on the brink of unpreparedness: "...there is plenty of evidence that defense cuts have gone too far. There are ample reports of spare parts shortages and cutbacks in training due to concerns about cost. It is also increasingly difficult to retain quality officers and senior enlisted personnel. In part this reflects the hot civilian job market, but surveys also indicate that frustration is high and morale is low in the armed forces."

Against this backdrop, AM General fell back into the uncertainty it regularly faced in the 1980s. Fighting for each year's bare minimum of Humvees became a fact of life. The company grew more grateful for the civilian version, too—civilian Hummers were keeping the military business afloat, the opposite of the problems that often had faced its ancestor companies during the 1950s and 1960s.

Bankrupty clouds

While AM General fought tooth and nail to preserve funding throughout the 1990s, it also faced corporate turmoil. In 1992, just as the Desert Storm boom was about to turn into the Clinton-era bust in South Bend, AM General's parent company was forced to put the company on the block to resolve a court order in its multi-billion-dollar bankruptcy proceedings.

LTV had been a vast conglomerate with diverse holdings, including AM General. The nation's 20th-largest defense contractor had logged $1.2 billion in sales to the Pentagon just prior to its bankruptcy; it also built fuselage sections for Boeing's 747, 757 and

767 jets on contracts that had lost money because of poor cost control. LTV had contracts to make missiles and rocket systems, and its aerospace division made stabilizers and airframes for the Air Force's B-2 "stealth" bomber and the C-17 cargo plane.

LTV's mistake had been in steel, entering the business just prior to the industry's severe downturn in the 1970s. Delinquent in pension contributions, LTV was ordered by a bankruptcy court to sell off its defense and aerospace divisions—with sales of $2 billion and 16,000 employees—in order to fund its pension plans and emerge from bankruptcy.

In 1992, LTV sold AM General to a New York company called Renco Group, which retained AM General name. Renco had bought a piece of LTV, one of the company's steel businesses, and had gotten to know AM General in the process.

Renco is the province of Ira Rennert, described by *Vanity Fair* as a "a short, heavy figure who walks slowly," a gentleman in his early seventies whom the magazine profiled during the contentious construction of his 100,000-square foot, 29-bedroom, 40-bath house in the Hamptons. The Renco Group, the magazine reported, was said to generate $2 billion a year though the company only operated through a dozen people in a 42nd-floor office at 30 Rockefeller Plaza in Manhattan. Renco Group's holdings mostly consist of mines and mills; *Vanity Fair* reports that Rennert is, through these holdings, the biggest private polluter in America. Rennert, according to the magazine, is also a generous benefactor of New York-area institutions of higher education: Rennert reportedly "gave $5 million to New York University's law school, $2.5 million to Barnard College, and millions more to Columbia and Yeshiva Universities, as well as to many Jewish causes. Rennert has remained a generous friend of its right-wing political leaders and the settlements they have encouraged."

Back in the field, though, AM General has considered itself fortunate to be scooped up by Rennert, for a reported $7.5 million. "Through the 1990s, when we made some money and didn't make some money, he put money into the Hummer," Mac Nab recalls. "The difference...whereas LTV was this huge conglomerate, Renco is an investment and holding company and hangs on to them. [Our president] Jim Armour gets things approved, but the owner always says, 'Jim, do what you think you ought to do.'"

Rennert's investment hasn't been high on returns until recently. In the mid-1990s, Rennert told AM General execs that he had "put a relatively small investment in company, and that investment is now worth negative $44 million," Mac Nab says.

Several times during the 1990s, it was assumed that AM General would be Renco's first bankruptcy. The drastic production cuts that followed Operation Desert Storm were conjoined with rising costs, and even the $100,000 Hummer couldn't generate enough profits to compensate. A second, more profitable product for consumers would have been a great addition to the lineup, and in fact AM General had talked about expanding its lineup, but its priorities were survival first, expansion later.

"We were in a fight for our lives," Armour said. "We just forgot about the next-generation Hummer."

Operation Restore Hope

The fight for lives never stopped for the Humvee's users, either. While at home it was the province of the wealthy, the celebrity and the self-made man, abroad the Humvee was going on international peacekeeping missions often lacking a defensive purpose, a criticism lodged repeatedly against the Clinton administration's foreign policy.

Somalia's desperate state in 1993, though, required some sort of international relief effort, and Clinton's assignation of U.S. troops to the United Nations' Operation Restore Hope was morally correct—a "vital humanitarian mission," in his words. A civil war and Africa's most persistent drought of the century had left 300,000 dead in the east African nation by 1992. A fragile truce had been brokered by the U.N., but looting and armed resistance to the relief workers plagued the operation from its inception.

Tribal and anti-U.N. hostility erupted on Oct. 3, 1993, when a hundred and twenty U.S. Army Special Operations Command soldiers—units of the Delta Force and Army Rangers commanded by Capt. Mike Steele —were dropped by helicopter into the capital of Mogadishu to apprehend two tribal leaders thought to be responsible for some of the resistance. U.S. forces clashed with Somali men, women and children supplied with automatic weapons and rocket-propelled grenades (RPGs) by Mohammed Farah Aidid, a Somali warlord.

The Battle of Mogadishu had begun, and in the next 24 hours, U.S. forces would lose 18 soldiers in an incident retold in the 2001 film *Black Hawk Down*. As soldiers landed in the middle of Mogadishu, the firefight became a mission to survive and to retrieve the victims of the crash of two Black Hawk helicopters in the more dangerous parts of the capital. And in that mission, the Humvee would be a hero of the second order, protecting U.S. soldiers intent on bringing back their own dead.

Spec. Dale Sizemore was one of the men dropped into Somalia in 1993. Today a college student in Illinois studying to be an elementary school teacher, Sizemore is best known as the man who cut a cast off his arm to join the fight. The story of the cast isn't glorious, he says: basically, Sizemore recalls, he had been trying to pin down a colonel prior to a volleyball game, scraped his elbow on a rope and got cellulitis and bursitis that needed protection to heal. Sizemore says he "absolutely hated the film" of the

War and Peace

The Humvee's history is inextricably linked to the two Iraqi wars.

Somali action at first—in part because the actor playing him (Matthew Marsden) was "a skinny guy, he didn't look anything like me"—but heaps praise on the 2,000 book by Mark Bowden that inspired the film.

Sizemore's drive led him to join with the most capable, highly trained force the Army fields. "I wanted to be a Ranger," he recalls. Ranger training turns soldiers into an elite fighting unit dropped into the cutting edge of battles—and it instills a distinct code of behavior into the 2000 or so active Rangers on duty at any time. "You put your life in their hands, and theirs in yours," Sizemore says. It's part of the Ranger creed: *Never shall I fail my comrades.*

"My experience with Humvees has been…lifesaving," Sizemore recalled on the tenth anniversary of the Battle of Mogadishu. "Without them we wouldn't have been able to bring the first two convoys of wounded back."

In many instances the Humvee was the deciding factor between life and death. Sizemore remembers one RPG attack in which the grenade went in a hole near a Humvee's gas tank and hit a can full of ammo. One soldier was killed; "The Humvee went back out that night." Another Humvee took an RPG in its door, and Sizemore says the window blew out instead of in, throwing the driver into the passenger seat, shaken but able to jump back behind the wheel and speed away.

In Mogadishu, Sizemore's Ranger training prepared him to save his own life and to rescue those who had died. Part of the seventh mission, his team made their way to the first Black Hawk crash site, where the pilots had landed between buildings. "We had to cut him in pieces to get him back home to his family," Sizemore says. "I was 21 years old at the time."

What had been planned as a 90-minute mission turned into a nearly day-long firefight that ended in 18 American dead and eighty-four wounded, as well as 350 to 1,000 Somali casualties. In the longer view, the action diminished the chances that the U.S. would again openly confront rogue nations, which left countries like Somalia, the Sudan, and Afghanistan open to civil unrest and covert terror operations like al-Qaeda. But the U.S. would send its troops into other arenas where the humanitarian situations were equally dire—into Haiti, Bosnia, Liberia and Kosovo.

The Somalian action would also have one critical aftereffect for AM General's Humvee. Humvees had functioned largely as troop and armament carriers in Mogadishu, but the loss of life convinced the Pentagon that an up-armored version of the war wagon was needed. Development would begin soon after troops departed Somalia, with production beginning by mid-decade.

Operation Uphold Democracy

Operation Restore Hope had sacrificed American lives for a noble goal. And in the course of the rout, the mission had burnished the Humvee's reputation for heroic service. In Haiti, the Humvee would play a different supporting role for a U.S. force that was sent to remove a dictator from power and restore democratic ideals—a mission that draped the Humvee across CNN's coverage but left even senior military befuddled by the Army's purpose under Clinton.

Haiti, the western third of the Caribbean island of Hispaniola, was and is one of the poorest countries in the western hemisphere. The six and a half million Haitians lived in wrenching poverty under the hand of the Duvalier father and son duo for much of the second half of the twentieth century. In 1986, anti-government protests chased Jean-Claude Duvalier into exile in France and led Haiti staggering down the path toward democracy but saddled with a military bent on subduing the democratic impulse.

After casting off the dictatorship of Jean-Claude Duvalier, the people of Haiti had elected a Catholic priest, Jean-Bertrand Aristide, to become their president on December 16, 1990, with 67 percent of the popular vote. Aristide presided as the first democratically elected leader of Haiti until a coup on September 29th, 1991, when Lieutenant General Raul Cedras took charge. Following the coup, political repression by the Haitian military against Aristide supporters resulted in over 3,000 deaths and caused thousands of Haitians to flee their country and head for the United States.

In July 1994, the United Nations Security Council authorized the United States to lead a multinational invasion of Haiti to drive out its military rulers. As President Clinton told America in a televised address on September 15, 1994, "The message of the United States to the Haitian dictators is clear: Your time is up. Leave now or we will force you from power."

Cedras refused to leave, but at the eleventh hour, a U.S. peace delegation sent by Clinton and led by former President Jimmy Carter, delivered the ultimatum that sent Cedras packing—leave or face a U.S. invasion. Cedras agreed to depart by October 15th; in the meantime, Operation Uphold Democracy began with the deployment of a U.S.-led coalition of more than 15,000 troops from America joined by symbolic handfuls of soldiers from nations like Bangladesh, Barbados, Guyana, Ghana, and Great Britain.

The justification, that action Haiti would promote democracy and prosperity, left open the question where the next dictatorship needing removal would be. The murky missions of these occasions brought critics from all over the media. Col. David Hackworth, *Newsweek's* defense contributor during the Haiti crisis and a talking head on Fox News, wrote in his weekly "Defending America" column in October 1994 that the Haiti mission had the hallmarks of other troubling interventions, mostly at the top:

I've been around warriors for 50 years, and the grunts we have in Haiti are the best I've seen. The soldiers and their small unit leaders—corporal to major—are dedicated, professional and know their jobs. The junior leaders bust their butts to look after the welfare of their men under terrible conditions.

This is not the case with the top army brass—lieutenant colonel to two-star general—from the U.S. Army 10th Mountain Division. From what I could see, these guys are not connected with the grunts at the bottom. Most are micromanaging every detail and are more interested in show than the welfare of their troops, which I learned long ago is a leader's sacred responsibility. They're so busy doing trivial stuff they miss the big picture.

An example: I was shooting the breeze with Air Force Master Sgt. Brian Sunday in a machine gun position overlooking the main gate at the airport. Two Jeep-like Humvees pulled up. Sunday said. "Oh, oh, here we go again."

A hand shot out of the second Humvee and punched the air. Brig Gen. George Close was "playing Patton again," raising hell with the troops and demanding they look good on TV, it seems his main job is to stage manage, making sure all his warriors wear their pots and flak jackets, sleeves rolled down, and look razor sharp in the boiling sun. Sure, guys in dangerous areas should wear all their protective gear, but, certainly not troopers in safe zones.

Close was so busy chewing on the NCO in charge, the sergeant, by now in shock, was too rattled to tell him that a Haitian standing right next to the Humvee had two grenades in his pocket...While Close was disciplining the troops, a grenade exactly like the ones in this guy's pocket was thrown in a downtown crowd, killing and wounding two dozen celebrating Haitians.

The 10th Division troops are unhappy. Haiti is desert hot and jungle humid. The mean temperature is 90 degrees, and with all the gear on, our warriors' body temperatures are somewhere between 100 and 110 degrees. Corporal Roger Leff, a 10th Division rifleman, says, "It's hotter than Somalia and Panama."

When asked, "Why are you wearing all that junk?" Leff answered, "It wouldn't look good if we wore shorts, floppy hats and rolled up our sleeves." Corporal Charles Hazelwood adds, "The brass are more concerned with what CNN shows than how we feel."

Our warriors wear essentially the same non-breathing uniforms their great-grandfathers cooked in during the Guadalcanal campaign in 1943. The Pentagon has stealth air- craft and satellite telephones, and the big brass—even in Haiti—have air-conditioned pads, just like the out-of-touch generals in Vietnam, a war that was lost by incompetent brass more interested in their careers than their troops.

Operation Allied Force/Joint Guardian

While at home, the Humvee continued to draw paparazzi, in the rest of the world it drew enemy fire. But in the aftermath of Mogadishu the Pentagon had ordered up-armored Humvees to be placed into service, and in years of intervention in the crumbling leftovers of Yugoslavia, the armored Humvees gave U.S. troops another weapon in the arsenal of democracy.

The path to armored Humvees was short and expedient. The Pentagon asked Fairfield, Ohio-based O'Gara-Hess & Eisenhardt and other armoring companies to submit prototypes for testing about a year after the Somalian operations had ended. O'Gara's version withstood the testing best, and the company won an initial contract for 59 armored Humvees that would find their first mission in the fractured Balkans.

The up-armored Humvee, known by the military as the M1114 is capable of stopping 7.62-mm armor-piercing rounds, and can withstand an overhead blast from a 155-mm artillery shell, according to O'Gara. The front end can endure the blast from a 12-pound land mine, the rear a four-pound mine. To date, more than 2900 of them have been placed in service, used mostly by military police, scouts, and field commanders in the line of fire from snipers, mines and other shifting threats.

The $150,000 M1114 debuted in Bosnia-Hercegovina, where war had broken out as Croatia and Serbia fought over territory that Croatia claimed as its own as it attempted to split from the former Yugoslavia. It was in Bosnia where, on a routine patrol, the first armored Humvee hit a land mine that blew the front end of the vehicle off–and saved the three military police inside.

The Croats and Serbs fought for most of the 1990s before Croatia asserted its independence. In a mostly ethnic Albanian province inside Serbia, though, the battle for freedom would end for some in mass graves. Kosovo had, under Tito's Yugoslavia, had a measure of self-rule and was 90 percent ethnic Albanian. But as Slobodan Milosevic assumed power in the remnants of the nation, attacks on the Kosovar Albanians grew more frequent and violent.

In 1998 one attack led to the deaths of 1500 Kosovars while Serb soldiers expelled more than 400,000 others from their homes. By the end of the spring, an estimated 1.5 million Kosovars, or about 90 percent of the region's population, had been forced out. Nearly a quarter-million Kosovar men were missing, and at least 5000 had been confirmed slaughtered.

Keen to keep the Balkans—namely, Albania and Macedonia—from completely disintegrating into chaos, the North Atlantic Treaty Organization (NATO) set the terms for Operation Joint Guardian in April 1999. Kosovo would be demilitarized, with NATO forces taking peacekeeping control, and refugees would be allowed to return to their homes.

Milosevic refused to comply, and on 23 March the order was given to commence air strikes. On 10 June 1999, after an air campaign lasting seventy-seven days, Milosevic relented and allowed a NATO peacekeeping force into Kosovo. Within weeks the Albanian Kosovars returned and the Serbian minority fled, essentially ceding the province to local rule. Milosevic then lost a re-election to Vojislav Kostunica in September of 2000, and though he initially would not accede to the results, he left office on Oct. 5, 2000. The butcher of the Balkans, who fought desperately to keep Serbia united, was arrested in his own country in 2001 and now faces an international tribunal in The Hague, on trial for crimes against humanity.

The end of the Clinton years had brought the Humvee full circle, from war wagon to peacekeeper and back. And as Clinton watched his legacy rebuked as George W. Bush defeated Al Gore in the 2000 general election in the most hotly contested election in a century, the ghosts of the last Bush administration, not vanquished by Bush nor by Clinton, appeared in the Humvee's sights again.

The end of the Gulf War had expelled Saddam Hussein from Kuwait, but it hadn't marked the end of his tyranny: it merely ushered in a new decade-long game of cat and mouse between Iraq and the United Nations—or more correctly, the United States and Great Britain, the only two members of the U.N. Security Council with the fortitude (and lack of Iraqi business connections) to promote and enforce a raft of resolutions.

After the war, the U.N. sent weapons inspectors to Iraq to search for weapons of mass destruction and the means of producing them, but Hussein would repeatedly block the mission. In 1991 the U.N. demanded Iraq destroy its weapons of mass destruction and pay Kuwait reparations before economic sanctions were lifted. In 1994 Iraq feinted a new invasion of Kuwait but backed off when the U.S. sent more than 50,000 troops to the region. In 1997, Iraq still had not disclosed its weapons programs per the U.N. resolutions that ended the war, and the following year, after Iraq sent U.N. weapons inspectors out of the country, President Clinton ordered a four-day bombing of Iraq in December.

Clinton's timing drew immediate suspension because of the near-parallel timing of discoveries that he had conducted an affair with White House intern Monica Lewinsky. The revelations brought Clinton eventually to the floor of the House of Representatives, where he was impeached for lying under oath about his conduct. While the Senate would fail to remove him from office for his actions, Clinton's credibility had evaporated. Half the nation saw his dalliance as no big thing—*relax, it's just sex*, in the title of a contemporary movie. The other half of the nation saw Clinton as a liar who lied under oath. His lack of self-control had tainted his entire eight-year administration, and in all likelihood cost his vice-president, Al Gore, the 2000 general election. It also later cost Clinton the ability to practice law in the U.S. Supreme Court, which disbarred him from its court on October 1, 2001.

HUMMER

SUV haters and bare cupboards

What the Clinton years had cost AM General could easily be tallied in lost dollars and the chance to expand by adding more Hummer-brand vehicles. But the circumstances worked in its favor in one way: for a while longer, Hummer would evade a potent enemy rising at home–the anti-SUV zealot.

In a decade of booming sales, the SUV had won millions of converts. And like any popular movement it made enemies, too. A backlash had begun, with the Sierra Club first among the green movement to find fault with SUVs for their gas mileage, their size, and their perceived elitism.

The likely trigger for the nascent outrage was unrealistically inexpensive gas. The American Petroleum Institute reported in 1999 that the two years prior had brought the cheapest gas on record. Cities like Atlanta saw a gallon of regular unleaded go for as little as 79 cents. But by February 1999, prices were still rising from a national average of $1.44 a gallon. Still, that price was only one cent higher than the adjusted price for 1972, and far less than the inflation-adjusted price of gasoline in 1981, which hit a record of $2.47.

During that relatively minor gas crunch the Sierra Club struck the first blow for the anti-SUV crowd by awarding the "Exxon Valdez Award" for environmental destruction to Ford. The reason? Its new heavy-duty Excursion SUV, which the green group dubbed "a rolling monument to environmental destruction," a "suburban supertanker," and a "suburban assault vehicle." Never mind that the Excursion was intended for fewer than 40,000 households a year, mostly those who towed boats, horse trailers and other lifestyle vehicles. The Sierra Club decided that the Excursion was appropriate for no one.

Riding the wake of the media hype already generated by gas prices, Sierra Club president Dan Becker took to the airwaves to

War and Peace

Low, low gearing in the transfer case is one reason Humvees are so capable off-road.

trash-talk the SUV and promote his organization's conspiracy theories of Detroit automakers hellbent on burning as much fuel as possible. Appearing on CNN's *TalkBack Live!*, Becker said gas-saving technologies were "sitting on the shelves in Detroit to make 50-, 60-mile-per-gallon cars...the technology exists. The auto industry has refused to put it on to the cars, and the Congress, which has taken $7 million in PAC contributions from the auto industry in just the past four years, is doing the auto industry's bidding by refusing to make the consumer's—put the consumers' interests first and the environment's interests first. And instead they're putting the oil sheiks and Saddam Hussein and the oil industry's profits first."

Becker had his facts wrong. While the technology existed to mate gas engines to electric motors and thus improve fuel economy, only Honda had made it to market. And even when it did reach the market, sales of the hybrid Honda Insight barely reached a level one tenth of the company's popular Civic compact—in no way recouping the hundreds of millions of dollars it no doubt cost to develop. Rather than develop a coherent agenda, like engaging automakers to develop fuel-efficient vehicles with grants, the Sierra Club and others began to beat on Detroit's automakers—as they had with electric vehicles—to build costly hybrids and incur the financial losses, regardless of public demand. In fact, the evidence pointed to the contrary: Americans didn't want electric vehicles, hybrid were untested, diesels had never gained much traction in America, and all the while, the big SUV continued to gain converts.

In fact, it was the largest SUVs that were seeing sales growth. The initial wave of modern SUVs in the early 1990s were mid-size vehicles based on smaller truck platforms. Chevrolet's Suburban was one large SUV that, due to strong sales throughout the 1990s, inspired a whole new set of competitors. Ford fielded its new Expedition in 1997, basing the full-size SUV off its F-150 truck platform, while Dodge introduced a Durango SUV that it sold as a super-sized alternative to the Explorer and Grand Cherokee. By the end of the decade Toyota would launch its own full-size SUV, the Sequioa. And even luxury brands like Cadillac and Lexus would get in on the high-profit act—all without the Sierra Club's permission and with customers' blessings.

But for Hummer, the move into large SUVs was no reason to celebrate. The contractor turned star maker had its civilian Hummer to sell—but lacked the resources to make another model devoted strictly to the glitterati.

Hummer was trapped in its own image. The legend had been burnished on the ground in Somalia, Haiti, and Kosovo as well as on the silver screen—the Humvee was as much a lead character in the cynical, stylized *Three Kings* (1999) as stars George Clooney and Mark Wahlberg and Ice Cube in the story about missing gold and the aftermath of Operation Desert Storm. *Black Hawk Down* (2001) had practically canonized the vehicles as not just a support player in warfare but an active combatant. Its role as a humanitarian vehicle had graced it with a slightly less aggressive public persona, but goodwill wasn't enough to convert the Hummer's great expectations into a financial windfall.

There was virtually no chance that AM General could go it alone in building a new vehicle distinct from the existing Hummer. The company had "dreamed a lot" about producing a second vehicle. But in the fiercely competitive U.S. market, it didn't just cost upwards of $500 million, if not a cool billion, to develop a new vehicle—it took innards of steel to sell it in a market where massive rebates and globally powerful marketing forces like General Motors, Ford and Toyota were already established players.

The complications of a smaller Hummer were myriad. "If we were going to make another vehicle, to make it smaller…never mind [the cost of] designing it. We'd have to build a new factory," Mac Nab points out.

The existing Hummer had shown AM General that engineering, building and marketing a civilian vehicle was even more of a headache than dealing with the Pentagon. The civilian sales were a necessity the company couldn't walk away from, though, in the lean Clinton years. "In the late 1990s things were pretty grim. The military program was operating at a loss," Mac Nab recalls. "The boss would say, if we didn't have the Hummer program we'd be out of business. The Humvee price would go up, and it would pass the price the Army was willing to pay."

Too, changing the Humvee to meet the more luxurious demands of civilians was out of the question. The Army didn't need a commercial interior, with leather or six-disc CD changers, more sound deadening, and cupholders. Taxpayer dollars developed the first Humvee—and since the military was happy with the vehicle's parameters, not much could change to make the Humvee more civilized.

"Throughout this period we had talked internally that the next official step would be a new generation vehicle very much like Jeep and somewhat like Range Rover," President Jim Armour said. "It would be designed specifically for the commercial market with some limited military application. We would actually reverse the roles with the Humvee."

But without a willing benefactor in the wings and without a massive bankroll of its own, AM General would have to wait until the right opportunity to use some other company's money came along. They had the cachet—but it would be up to the world's largest automaker to see the potential in the Hummer and take on the duty of turning it into a mass-marketed object of lust, envy and greed.

Chapter 6

GM Wants In

"General Motors certainly needs to change. We can't do business the way we used to."—**GM Chairman Jack Smith, at the 2000 North American International Auto Show where GM unveiled its new HUMMER concept.**

AM General's savior came in the form of the world's biggest automaker in 1999. When building its own Hummer seemed out of reach, General Motors approached the company with the right amount of savvy and deference and won a its own competition for the rights to build the new HUMMER brand into something far more than the Humvee-cum-Hummer had become.

Two emerging trends fueled big change in the U.S. auto market at the turn of the century—the twenty-first, not the twentieth. And in both cases, they directly influenced General Motors' decision to pursue—and to buy—the rights to build HUMMERs of its own.

HUMMER

Across Detroit, Tokyo and Stuttgart, the biggest phenomenon by far in the 1990s hadn't been hybrid vehicles, though they were starting to attract more attention than the feeble electric vehicles made by GM and Ford to satisfy the letter of the law in California. Those pure electrics had clearly failed—and the EV1 alone cost GM an estimated $500 million. Now hybrids were beginning to make a stir, and in pointed contrast to the massive SUVs coming from Detroit, Toyota and Honda had introduced cars that used a combination of gas and electric power to boost fuel economy—and they'd priced them below $20,000. The loss leaders, which got 48 and 68 miles per gallon respectively, had already paid back their enormous development costs in enormously good public relations.

Neither had the big newsmaker been the re-emergence of what designers like to call "heritage" vehicles. Fumbling the design leadership had cost Detroit dearly in the 1980s and with new vehicles like the Ford Thunderbird and Chrysler PT Cruiser, the domestics were clearly intent on recapturing the aura of vehicles that lived and breathed the style of another era. Even Germany's Volkswagen got in on the act with the New Beetle, essentially a mimeograph of the 1970s-era Bugs grafted on the body of a modern Golf compact.

These cars drew crowds at auto shows, but when it came to the big story of the decade in the auto industry, the arguments clearly went to the business side of the story—mergers and acquisitions. Chrysler went first: in 1998 it sold itself to Mercedes-Benz' parent company for what was argued a paltry $36 billion. Chrysler had been through several boom and bust eras, and had promised that, after a government bailout in 1981, it had reengineered itself to resist future downturns. And yet when the suitors came sniffing, Chrysler Corporation did the wise thing and took the best offer it could get, at the absolute peak of the M&E market. Daimler-Benz hadn't looked too closely at the company's dwindling passenger-car sales or the looming intrusions of the Japanese into Chrysler's fat profits in the minivan and truck arenas, either. At the time, Chrysler chairman Bob Eaton was derided as a sellout and a coward—but flash-forward to 2003, and Chrysler's 25,000 job cuts and DCX's sinking stock values now make Chrysler look like a company that sold at the perfect height of an otherworldly market valuation.

Crosstown—or really, downstate—rival Ford took the ball from the newly minted DaimlerChrysler in 1999 and rolled with it in force. Ford was flush with cash, and behind gutsy, spendthrift Chairman Jac Nasser, the company decided the future of the car industry lay in the premium brands and in the service side of the business. Already part-owner of Mazda and full keyholder of Aston Martin and Jaguar, Ford sat down for a prolonged buying binge first by sewing up the rights to Britain's Land Rover in March of 2000 for what seemed a paltry $2.8 billion. DaimlerChrysler already had one venerable nameplate in the booming sport-utility vehicle niche in Jeep—and now Ford had captured the other available nugget of historical importance in the niche.

The biggest fully developed trend, though, was the takeover of the car market by trucks—not just SUVs, but pickups and minivans as well. At the beginning of the decade carmakers were selling a million SUVs a year. By the end of 1999, that figure had tripled.

But why bother for a vehicle that might only be worth 50,000 units? GM and the rest of Detroit were beginning to see models crumble. The marketing types call it fragmentation – companies that could count on selling 400,000 vehicles of one basic type were now being pressed to splinter models. Instead of a basic family sedan, the same "intenders" now could be wooed by a wagon, an SUV, even a four-door pickup truck.

GM was being left out of the meat of the market, though, and especially when it came to luxury SUVs, the General was left wanting. Long ago, before the Explorer existed, GM had mocked up a four-door version of the Blazer mid-size SUV, which eventually would go into production. But when first shown to then-GM Chairman Roger Smith, famous for starting the Saturn brand and leading GM's forays into diversification, Smith apocryphally told the presenters of the proposal, *Who would want a four-door truck, anyway?*

Nonetheless, the General's SUV fleet would grow exponentially during the 1990s to include very well designed Suburbans, and a new mid-size Chevrolet/GMC/Oldsmobile SUV with all the right stuff to take on Ford's juggernaut Explorer where GM's prior offerings hadn't even been competitive with the oldest Mitsubishi Monteros. The problem was that GM's vehicles lacked spark. None of them carried the ritzy, capable connotations that a Range Rover parked in a Ford exec's driveway did. Even a Jeep Rubicon said more about its owner than the average Suburban, much less the pint-sized Chevy Tracker or the fairly abominable two-door Chevy Blazer. In 1998, Ford turned its Expedition into a ritzy, high-profit Lincoln Navigator and promptly stole GM's thunder in the luxury market, though a revised Escalade would put Caddy back in the hip-hop crowd's graces within a few years.

GM execs knew the problem—and at least a few of them thought the answers would be too costly to put into place. Push GMC way upmarket and risk losing thousands of sales? Or simply leave the very top of the SUV market to other brands and focus on pumping out more Tahoes? By the end of 1999, GM and its cadre of young execs (young by GM standards—even CEO Rick Wagoner was 53 by the time he took charge of the company's North American operations) looked to Indiana for the answer.

Fighting for the right to sell HUMMERs would be a sub rosa battle among Detroit's automakers. And though AM General's executives will not speak the names of the companies that expressed interest in taking over the brand, it's logical to assume that each of Detroit's automakers was interested in capturing the HUMMER's lightning for itself.

Chrysler had the most logical connections to develop a future HUMMER, considering that its Jeep brand was a distant cousin of AM General to begin with. The Chrysler lineup of SUVs and trucks already leaned toward testosterone-riffing models like the Peterbilt-like Dodge Ram, and Chrysler more than the larger Detroit makes, operated in smaller vehicle niches with lesser expectations for vehicle volume. Its Ram pickup, for example, made huge strides in sales from the day it introduced the 1994 model, but the volume still was half of GM and Ford's big truck sales of more than 750,000 units a year. But Chrysler was about to be swallowed itself, by Germany's Daimer-Benz, and the prospect of integrating into the new DaimlerChrysler and gaining two other luxury SUVs, the Mercedes ML-Class and the G-Class, as corporate cousins would almost make a new Chrysler HUMMER an unnecessary financial risk.

Ford, too, was on a buying spree, having acquired Jaguar and Aston Martin in the late 1980s and showing interest in swallowing more brands. The company's CEO Jac Nasser expressed interest in moving Ford's portfolio away from its core operations and reaching into the luxury realm. And indeed before long, Ford had purchased Volvo and Land Rover to round out its European portfolio. Those acquisitions would bring indigestion of their own, but between Land Rover and Ford's strong lineup of SUVs in nearly every niche, a HUMMER project may have been seen as a distraction from the business at hand—which, as it turned out, would be neglecting Ford's passenger car business for years. Ford had consummated a

HUMMER

Civilian HUMMERs are equally as capable as their military cousins when the road comes to an end.

sought-after deal with Harley-Davidson to badge its pickups with the Harley logo, though, so the model for a HUMMER deal existed.

General Motors had the greatest need to flesh out its SUV portfolio, and already had some linkage with AM General, having sold it an engine design in the early days of the civilian Hummer. GM had the least competitive lineup of SUVs of the American brands by the end of the 1990s. The company's image had been built on fantastic cars—Bel Air, Corvette, Cadillac—and though its Suburban had been a strong seller, it lacked the runaway SUV sales hit that both Ford and Chrysler possessed. GM could have used a Jeep in its lineup, but in its long history of tail fins, chrome, and horsepower, it had lacked the strong off-road brand to complement its passenger-car business when the time came.

The epic shift in American taste to SUVs changed GM's mind, just as surely as GM's complex internal issues. Rising star and CEO Rick Wagoner knew that GM needed big income to overcome a looming pension funding problem, and the company's stale car lineup was losing customers by the day. A successful high-dollar truck could plug several holes in the GM lineup and bring in lots of easy cash, while helping to fund a new generation of passenger cars that might be more competitive with Japanese and German brands.

What ultimately drew GM to HUMMER was the image, the potential, and in some part, the company's reliance on alliances, not mergers or takeovers. While Chrysler auctioned itself off and Ford spent billions to own European brands outright, GM structured new businesses with a slew of Asian makers to limit its risk and maximize the potential for sharing platforms, engines, and product development expertise. GM bought a 20-percent stake in Subaru, eventually twinning the brand with its Saab luxury brand to cut development costs; likewise, GM teamed with Suzuki to buy Korea's bankrupt Daewoo and gain entry into the closed Korean market as well as supply GM with new, profitable small cars to be sold in the U.S.

So when it came time to approach AM General about HUMMER, General Motors likely was the only American company with the right relationship in mind, one that would appeal to the smaller company and one that would cost General Motors far less than buying it outright, also taking on military contracts GM had no real interest in winning. The way to build more HUMMERs, GM and AM General would decide, would be to form an alliance that gave AM General the means to build its own company up and GM, a key to the piece of the luxury SUV audience it was missing.

Who's on, first?

Even within General Motors, the genesis of the HUMMER brand is up for grabs. Two top execs claim the idea as their own.

"I had approached a number of people about getting the rights to the brand," says GM's Wayne Cherry, director of design when the company made its first play for HUMMER. An Art Center College of Design grad, he joined the company's advanced design studios in 1962 and was attached to the team that styled the evocative, swooping 1966 Oldsmobile Toronado, one of GM's finest efforts of the 1960s, and the first Chevy Camaro, a musclecar with a shelf life that would almost span as long as his career at GM, which culminated in his retirement on January 1, 2004.

Cherry took the helm at GM Design during a time when the company's reputation for styling was as battered as its share price. The General had flirted with bankruptcy the year before—and the product pantry was nearly bare, thinly populated by uncompetitive vehicles like the tepid Saturn S-Series and the slab-sided Pontiac Aztek. But before tackling the major portfolio problems, Cherry had his first encounter with the Humvee.

The tall, lean head stylist at the world's largest automaker says his interest in the Humvee dates back to the days of Operation Desert Storm, when he was stationed in Germany. Cherry had spent much of career in Europe.

"I was living in Germany at the time," he recalls. "They were quite often on the Autobahn in convoys. That's where I was really familiar with them."

"[It] was on television so much," he recalls. "It sort of featured Hummers. We talked about televising the war and the featuring of the Hummer, that it would have a huge influence on how people would respond to Hummer after the war, particularly civilian Hummers."

Cherry carried his fascination back to the States, where he would assume the mantle of head GM stylist in 1992. As Hummer sold civilian versions, Cherry says he and other GM execs were talking about what could be done with the brand as early at 1997, "because I had been fascinated with what we could do with the brand."

Cherry says he discussed the idea of doing a commercialized Hummer "with a number of people, including [former GM North America chief Ron] Zarrella. To my knowledge, in the discussions I had with Ron, I was the one who initiated it…I was really the first one that really starting talking about the possibility."

Cherry's role as chief designer gave him the leeway to begin exploring a militaristic vehicle. "I had one of the designers do some sketches, showing how we could develop Hummer vehicles from current components…partly because of my interest, partly because of aspects in the market, militaristic types of products." The trend not only touched autos, Cherry says, but showed up in clothes, media and other consumer items.

GM's Advanced Product Exploration (APEX) studios would be the home to the ur-Hummer sketches that gradually evolved into a concept prototype that would ring the bells. "We had a number of militaristic vehicles and built some full-size models—not HUMMERs.

But "as a piece of product design, it was fascinating to me. We could capture the visual essence but we would need the HUMMER brand to do it properly." Doing it right meant keeping the Humvee's patina—the extreme side of the vehicles, its narrow grille and its feral stance.

While Cherry says he pressed and discussed with other execs on acquiring the rights to the HUMMER brand, his annual responsibility in preparing concept vehicles for display at auto shows drew near. Of the various auto shows in North America, only a handful attract the attention of international press. Those in Chicago, New York, and Los Angeles often woo a million curious citizens of their cities, some interested in buying, some merely interested in poking and prodding the newest vehicles.

Of them all, the annual North American International Auto Show, held each January in Detroit, is the most important. It's the domestics' turf—and their chance to show off for 8,000 media from all around the globe. It's where new Mustangs and Corvettes are christened, and the stunts used to introduce new American vehicles have ranged from the clever to the physically unimaginable. They have included driving a Jeep Grand Cherokee through a plate-glass window; catapulting a Chrysler minivan across a stage; and hauling in diva-for-hire Celine Dion to warble for a charity preview. The largest displays at the show easily cost tens of millions of dollars—and are dismantled after just three weeks of media previews and show days.

Being best in show at Detroit can set the stage for favorable coverage through the often difficult two to three years a vehicle takes to go from a concept to an actual drivable, saleable vehicle. Total surprise seems to works well—as Volkswagen found in 1994

War doesn't often take place on open fields: Humvees are used to patrolling highways and freeways to defend freedom.
Courtesy of AM General

The Humvee uses a ladder frame for strength and durability.

Courtesy of AM General

Slimming down the center console was the major achievement of the H1's 2004 interior remodeling. *Courtesy of General Motors*

HUMMER owners can sign up for a driving academy on AM General grounds, where instructors teach them the finer points of rock climbing and mud running. *Courtesy of General Motors*

Lots of ground clearance makes certain the Humvee won't be stopped in its tracks. *Courtesy of AM General*

On patrol or in heavy combat, the Humvee delivers.
Courtesy of AM General

Humvees are designed to fit into different military shipping containers, including aircraft carriers and helicopters.
Courtesy of AM General

Marine headquarters in Baghdad—Ground Zero for Humvee history buffs. *Courtesy of AM General*

The four-door ragtop HUMMER H1—at home in the desert or on the beach. *Courtesy of General Motors*

In the span of a decade, Schwarzenegger took himself and the HUMMER brand from Hollywood to Sacramento.
Courtesy of General Motors

The HUMMER H2 SUT concept debuted at the New York auto show in 2001, just months before terrorists took down the city's World Trade Center towers. *Courtesy of General Motors*

The HUMMER concept's interior was a work in progress, literally until the moment the vehicle was unveiled to the press at the Detroit Auto Show in 2000. *Courtesy of General Motors*

The finished product: GM's Hummer H2. The H2 incorporates the rigid frame and boxy look of the original Hummer and H1 with the clean lines of the modern SUV. *Courtesy of General Motors*

Fording is, ironically, one of the GM HUMMER's more notable talents.
Courtesy of General Motors

HUMMER dealerships often incorporate an outdooer showroom, and sometimes an off-road course, to demonstrate its capabilities.
Courtesy of General Motors

Another day at the office at the HUMMER Driving Academy.
Courtesy of General Motors

when they showed the Concept 1, which would mark the company's return to its Beetle roots and a dramatic uptick in sales.

In 1999, Cherry saw the crop of show vehicles being readied for Detroit, and thought the crew could use one more. "I told Ron that what we ought to do is build an H2 concept model for Detroit," he says, to capture the excitement of the show crowds for a business deal that hadn't even been arranged or consummated. His reasoning: "I we start the concept and we're not successful [with a HUMMER deal], then all we've lost is the time on the concept." Cherry brought the idea to GM's strategy board and made his pitch—and in the latter part of 1999, his studio was charged with the task of a concept that could eventually be the son of Hummer.

Another GM exec also lays claim to being the proud papa of the HUMMER brand.

Mike DiGiovanni is HUMMER's general manager—which, within the General Motors monolith, means he's responsible for steering the brand against its competition. If you think the leader of HUMMER would be a brash iconoclast incapable of speaking in anything less than exclamatory sentences, you'd be wrong. Slight of frame and soft-spoken, DiGiovanni is as measured and mild-mannered as the Humvee is brash.

DiGiovanni started at GM in 1979 as an economist, running corporate research and studying where General Motors would and should be in future trucks. As leader of industry truck forecasting, he took over a plum assignment as leader of a new market intelligence group in 1998 charged with the duty of getting GM back into a leadership role in the auto world.

That leadership had been sorely tested since the 1970s. Aside from the occasional hit, GM's product portfolio in the mid-1990s was long on mediocrity and short on brilliance. The Corvette was improving, and the Seville STS gave Cadillac a glimpse into the revival it's currently experiencing. But GM's lineup was overpopulated with average or less than average vehicles like the Saturn S-Series, in theory a competitor for the Honda Civic and Toyota Corolla but in practice, much coarser and kludgier.

Pontiac's first attempt at a crossover vehicle was the nadir of GM product development in the eyes of many consumers. Introduced in 2001, the Aztek started life as a decent GM minivan, rebodied in the hopes of catching more youthful buyers with an appealing exterior and a reconfigurable interior made for outdoor sports. What resulted was a study in design by committee: the body scarred by ridges and cutlines, possibly one of the least attractive vehicles ever to issue from the same studios that created the 1955 Chevrolet Bel Air and the 1966 Corvette Sting Ray.

So in 1998, GM tapped DiGiovanni to lead a market intelligence group that could help GM get the right kinds of new vehicles to market more quickly. "GM was missing a lot of trends," DiGiovanni admits. But the group's task has begun to show fruit: the 2002 Chevrolet Avalanche, a truck with a reconfigurable bed, was one vehicle to come from the group.

Another was, in a way, the GM HUMMER. The group had done marketing studies to gauge what trends were fueling new shoppers to turn to import or other domestic brands at the expense of GM. DiGiovanni and the group found that the people they studied—particularly younger people—were interested in vehicles with militaristic styling or themes. So much so, that GM began working on a vehicle that came to be known as the "Chunk," a two-door, relatively small vehicle that didn't even wear the HUMMER seven-slot grille in conceptual form.

The Chunk was based on GM's mid-size SUV architecture, and had a small pickup bed off the back instead of a cargo area. While the research showed the shape was well-received, an interesting thing happened when it wasn't given a GM badge.

The idea was that the Chunk would be tested to varying degrees of butchness, with different brand names applied. When the HUMMER name was applied, it "went through the roof," DiGiovanni says. "we were shocked how well it did when it was a HUMMER." Other brand names were coming up. "we put GMC on it, put Land Rover on it. Even Land Cruiser, since Toyota was playing around with some militaristically-styled vehicles." Some respondents identified it properly as a future HUMMER–many in one test market, because a local pizza place used a HUMMER as their delivery vehicle.

Why HUMMER? "It was obvious young people had a fascination from Desert Storm," he says. "HUMMER is the number one selling miniature die cast. It's outselling Lamborghini and the 'Vette."

But it could also have been from the maturation of the sport-utility vehicle market. "The fact is that all SUVs were beginning to look alike. The Jeep Wrangler had been very successful with a somewhat militaristic style. It's a potential trend, we thought, so let's test it."

The other trend was the emergence of luxury SUVs. In 1998, Ford took its full-size Expedition SUV, added a vertical grille and luxury touches inside and dubbed it the Lincoln Navigator. "We saw this luxury SUV thing could take off...why not a son of HUMMER?"

To that point, Hummer only had the $100,000 Hummer to sell, and at only 700 to 800 copies a year going to civilians, it wasn't accessible. DiGiovanni was convinced that Hummer could work as a brand with multiple vehicles. And he didn't want to miss out on the potential to other companies, such as Ford, that might be interested in doing the same thing. "I don't know this for a fact, [AM General CEO] Jim Armour keeps that close to his vest, but other companies were interested. We beat them to the punch."

"GM did the right thing from the beginning," Armour told auto journalists John Lamm and Matt DeLorenzo in 2002. "Mike DiGiovanni called me requesting a meeting and said they would like to come to us. Some of the other companies asked us to come to them. It's a small thing, but to us it was very significant."

As soon as DiGiovanni's team identified the trend, he rushed to take it to GM's North American strategy board in January of 1999. he presented it to the strategy group headed by Ron Zarrella, GM's president of North American operations who was brought in 1994 by then chairman John G. Smale, a Procter & Gamble executive.

Now chairman and CEO at eyecare company Bausch & Lomb, Zarrella was the champion of brand management at GM. He thought GM's success would lie not within its brand names but within individual vehicles as brands: Corvette was a prime example. Under Zarrella, divisional advertising was all but eliminated, since he declared that the real brands were products like the Olds Alero or Pontiac Aztek. Zarrella was one of a slew of execs GM sought from the outside in the 1990s to turn around the way it developed and marketed vehicles. Zarrella's prior experience at Proctor & Gamble seemed to give him the edge in transforming GM's glut of divisions into clear-cut marketing niches. And indeed, his legacy includes some divisional realignment that, in part, helped Cadillac secure the funding for a $4 billion new range of vehicles designed to catapult it back into the top leagues of international cars.

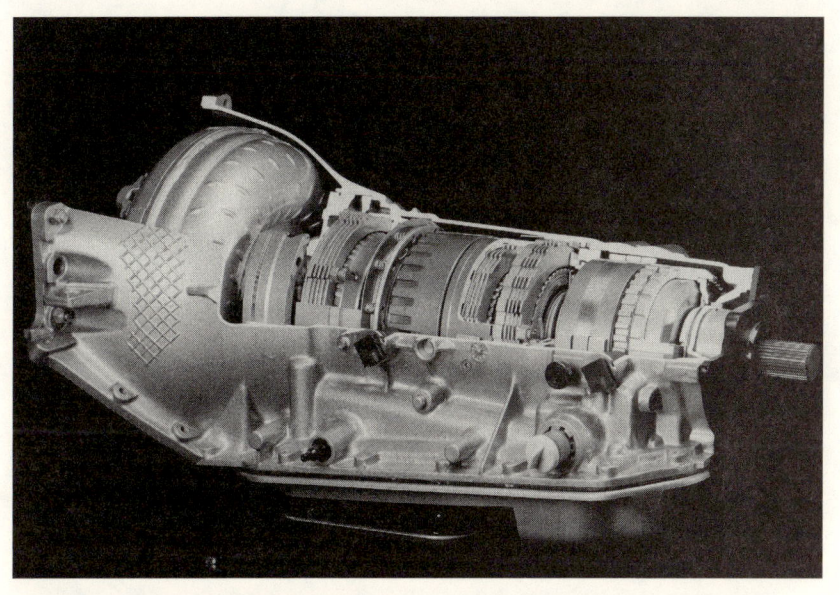

Built for extreme duty, the Humvee shares parts with its civilian cousin—except the gun turret.

Zarrella's downfall at GM came when market share continued to decline, even in the face of investing hundreds of millions of dollars in brands like now-defunct Oldsmobile. His "brand mantra" had convinced GM that it could revive its market share at least to more than 30 percent of the U.S. market. At the time Zarrella left in November of 2001, GM's market share was preparing to register its first increase in 30 years—far off its historic heights of the mid-1960s, but given the heated competition in the U.S. market, a heartening sign of stabilization.

His critics were gathering long before he resigned from GM in 2001. "You can't sell cars and trucks like you were selling contact lenses," said John Z. DeLorean, the scandal-tainted former Pontiac exec that went on to infamy with his own company, his own sportscar, and his own drug scandal. "To the average buyers, a car is second only to his home as the most significant purchase in a lifetime."

To his credit Zarrella liked the initial concept of going after HUMMER—but not the notion of transforming the one civilian vehicle into a range of vehicles to compete with Chrysler's Jeep. That January, DiGiovanni's team presented three ideas. "The first two did not do well," he recalls. But the third one rang Zarrella's bell: to buy the HUMMER brand, but not the company. Zarrella "jumped on it. He got it immediately and told me to go down to South Bend and pitch it to Jim Armour."

DiGiovanni credits GM's market-research in identifying the possibility of the HUMMER brand. And when his team set foot in South Bend, Ind., he wasn't at all certain that the concept would go over. "We presented the research in 20 minutes," he says, "and Armour didn't saw a word." After a minute or two went by, DiGiovanni remembers, "He said, 'Hell yeah, it's a great idea. We'd been thinking the same thing.'"

The art of the deal

AM General had already studied how it might build another vehicle, a commercial vehicle that would even out its business portfolio. They had planned on how they could expand the plant to build a steel-bodied vehicle, and what the vehicle might be like—but until GM's full-on press, no overtures had progressed to any serious stage.

Both Cherry and DiGiovanni believe the deal wouldn't have happened for a few factors—for the fact that GM came to AM General and didn't summon them to Detroit, for example. Critical, too was the fact that the concept vehicle was already well underway. After the initial contacts, "Jim was pretty excited how far along we were on the exterior and interior concept models," Cherry says.

But the deal was far from done when the team of execs left Indiana. The idea was to get the HUMMER name by license, and put it on a utilitarian, militaristic truck. AM General wasn't interesting in a licensing agreement—they were interested in building the trucks. Armour and company asked GM's team to figure out how to structure it and come back to them: "We began immediately to sell them on the story that if it makes sense to acquire the HUMMER brand because of what it is, it makes even more sense to use the company that created the truck and use the same workforce."

The idea went dark for a while, until about a month later when the owner of AM General's parent company Renco, Ira Rennert, asked GM for a meeting in New York to revive talks. Rennert asked GM representatives to consider AM General building the new HUMMER for GM under license.

GM responded by sending a team of truck engineering executives to Indiana to find out what AM General had to offer, and how to interface with GM's huge staff. Ken Lindensmith, a lifer at GM with most of his experience at GMC, had some military background in dealing with competing on contracts for the armed services. One of the team that went to figure out how a GM/AM General partnership would work, Lindensmith saw early that AM General had some clear ideas about how a possible joint-venture could work, logistically and physically.

"They had done some scraping of the surface as to how they would do it," he says. "We went to their Mishawaka plant, and they walked us through plans as to how to expand the plant for an all-steel body. They had some pretty good ideas. So I came back to Detroit and put together a framework of a proposal we took to AM General.

Soon after, a meeting of the minds was held in the mud between the two groups near Lexington, Ky. While discussing the potential spin-off of a HUMMER vehicle from GM's full-size SUVs, Lindensmith and the GM team wanted to convince AM General that "we knew something about off-road trucks. We set up a drive program and went down to Kentucky; they brought Hummers, we brought GMT820s (full-size SUVs) as well as a couple of pickups, to show our five-link suspension as well as the truck's leaf-spring suspensions.

"At the end of the day, our vehicles went almost everywhere theirs went, theirs went almost everywhere ours went. In some cases, in narrow spots, we got the Hummer bodies wedged in. They were pretty impressed, in terms of our vehicles' articulation. Then, literally, all of the Hummer drivers got into their vehicles and drove them home. All ours had fairly extensive body damage: crushed rocker panels, dented doors, from $300 to $700 a vehicle."

The demonstration had convinced AM General of GM's seriousness and depth of product. And it led them to another meeting in Detroit that ended in a handshake deal that put GM and AM General into an exclusive negotiating phase that would protect GM as it began to get some HUMMER ideas of its own.

The basics of the deal combined the strengths of both companies, Lindensmith says. GM's excellence lay in project engineering—figuring out what a vehicle can be, assembling it from a vast parts bin of components, everything from fasteners to entire drivetrains used in markets around the world, and an equally vast distribution network and a ready-to-cherry-pick dealer network experienced in selling both heavy-duty trucks and luxury vehicles. AM General could offer a few unique benefits: a union labor force paid less than those UAW workers at General Motors' plants, and an area viable for a new assembly plant, plus proximity to Detroit.

Duly impressed and with a vision for the agreement, Lindensmith returned—and Armour came to Detroit next, in April of 1999, to meet with a wider GM team. At the end of the meeting, GM asked Armour to sign an exclusive agreement, ending what were fairly serious discussions with at least one other automaker. Both companies had entertained the notion of GM buying AM General, which was ruled out because of the vastly different cultures and scope of business. A joint venture was ruled too cumbersome. A unique licensing agreement was the way GM packaged the deal to appeal to AM General.

By the early part of May, the deal was fairly well in place. GM would manage all the engineering for the project, and buy all the parts, with AM General charged with assembling the vehicle. GM would help AM General with an interest-free loan with which they would construct a new assembly plant, while guaranteeing that GM owned the HUMMER name lock, stock and barrel. GM would distribute the vehicle through its dealers. AM General would earn a licensing fee for each vehicle it built, which in turn paid off the loan from GM. The deal would run through 2009, and even then, AM General would receive "special consideration" for the second generation of HUMMER product due in that year.

GM would not be limited in the number of HUMMER models it could develop, nor in the number it could build. It would also have the right to build more vehicles beyond the amount AM General's plant could produce in Mishawaka.

The financial incentives were unusual and even within GM, some execs murmured that the terms were generous to AM General, particularly the loan. Lindensmith counters: "We owned the HUMMER name in December 1999 before we paid AM General one dollar in any assembly fees —about three years before. We both share risk in the vehicle…how it's marketed makes a big difference, quality makes a big difference." Within another month, AM General had committed with its labor force to build the vehicle through 2009.

GM and AM General announced publicly in June of 1999 that they would work together on future projects, without divulging that a concept vehicle already was in progress. Most of the press discussion centered on the existing Hummer, and what GM could do with it. Some correctly predicted GM would build a baby HUMMER.

And in the interim, Mike DiGiovanni became the first head of what would become the newly minted HUMMER division, asked by Zarrella since it was his idea. Zarrella didn't believe in DiGiovanni's sweeping plans for a full division–according to DiGiovanni, he still saw it as more of a niche product. Then DiGiovanni ran into him in the restroom and said, "we gotta talk." Zarrella, DiGiovanni says, thought it was "pretty grandiose," a powerful brand but a niche product–but reluctantly agreed to the vision. "Either you're going to fall flat on your face or you're going to succeed with it," Zarrella told him.

In April GM had approached AM General with the serious idea–but it wasn't until December 22, 1999, that the official deal became public. In the interim a memorandum of understanding gave the companies the legal cover to begin more serious work in converting the principles of the Chunk and AM General's own ideas into a concept vehicle for the Detroit auto show.

Keeping it real

Possibly the most difficult task of all lay ahead of the GM team responsible for translating the butch Humvee personality into a smaller, slightly more civilized large SUV. It could be smaller and less powerful, but no less imposing nor any less capable. "It couldn't be a rebadged Tahoe," DiGiovanni echoes from research in study clinics. "It had to look like a Hummer and perform like a Hummer off-road." The capability of the vehicle, the audience to which it was aimed, all were important, but the look was everything.

The semantics were critical in giving GM's HUMMER its authenticity, he says. In GM's past there were too many examples of taking an idea and fitting it to the mechanicals on hand. Most disastrously, Cadillac had taken a Chevrolet Cavalier—a *Cavalier*—in 1982, trimmed it with leather and slapped on a large grille and called it the Cimarron. It was a low point of GM's once-lauded product development. If DiGiovanni and his team had taken the Hummer look and simply applied it across an SUV lineup, "it would have bombed," he is convinced. "The whole world was expecting us to do a rebadged Tahoe."

The question of how much Hummer to translate into GM's HUMMER division wasn't easy or simple. The planar sides of the vehicle—meant to make it slimmer for access to off-road locations—its vertical windshield (in the military vehicles, done so the trucks wouldn't reflect light and reveal the military position) and the five-link rear suspension were identified as critical elements to HUMMER's "DNA."

DNA is a term now thrown around in Detroit almost as much as at the CDC. Brands have DNA, individual vehicles like

HUMMER

the Corvette have DNA, and the buyers who shop specific vehicles are interested in unwinding that DNA and intertwining it with their own. Even for companies with established DNA—or more loosely, brand heritage—it's expensive to make the right decisions for brand character. Ford's efforts at Jaguar have been a virtual test bed for the theories of integrating tiny brands into massive companies and doing it while preserving character. "Ford had to invest a lot in Jaguar to make authentic Jaguars," DiGiovanni admits. "At the beginning they certainly did."

The essentials of what would become the GM HUMMER would shake out pretty quickly in a torrent of marketing research, engineering input and gut instinct. As styling clinics with consumers pointed out quickly, it wasn't an easy thing to make a real HUMMER. When shown a series of concepts progressively more extreme—more HUMMER, if you will—interest increased. The sketches (really compositions made from data generated by computerized models within GM Design) got butcher and the reactions grew more intense. "The one that was the most "Hummer" went through the roof," DiGiovanni recalls.

There was some confusion over whether GM intended to replace the original HUMMER or make a smaller vehicle in the mid-size SUV category. GM had been shooting for a vehicle in the high $40,000 range (the base truck would come out around $48,000). And the further GM distanced the HUMMER from its existing trucks in terms of equipment, tooling changes, radical sheetmetal departures and aggressive off-road cues, the more of a hit it became for test audiences. "It would cost you more money," he says, "but you could make more money too."

While GM stylist Clay Dean was set to work out clay models and develop the look, DiGiovanni and his team kept close touch with consumer surveys. The concept and later, the production vehicle that

GM Wants In

While the H2 isn't known for its speed, the 316 horsepower and 360 ft-lbs of torque it puts out are more than adequate to deal with any terrain.

would come from this early work would be the most market researched vehicle in the history or General Motors. "We conducted more product clinics, I'm positive, than in the history of general motors to get it right," DiGiovanni says.

Part of the reason so much was studied was that, already, working with AM General was perceived as a sure thing—but one that GM would have plenty of opportunity to bungle.

'The last time GM had done this was ten years ago, with Saturn," says Marc Hernandez, an affable giant of a man, has been working with HUMMER since before it was a division, in 1999. A former teacher at Northern Michigan University in psychology and education, would be responsible for honing the marketing principles behind the HUMMER idea. He says he thought at the time he was first approached to join the study group for HUMMER. "If we blew this, we would have done what everybody expected would be done: 'GM screwed it up.'"

The pressure began to build from everywhere—automotive publications, daily newspapers like the *Wall Street Journal*, even the competition. "Chrysler obviously has an interest in off-road vehicles," Hernandez says. "And some of the off-road publications thought GM had no off-road experience. It's a little but like playing poker, knowing what your cards are and everybody thinking you had a bad hand.

But Hernandez and others knew if they did the vehicle right, the right kind of buyers would come—a lucrative pool of buyers that were leaving GM for other vehicles and other brands. Identifying those buyers became Hernandez' task and finding out how much Hummer magic needed to rub off on to GM, the difficult calculus.

One of the ways GM studies potential new vehicles is through psychographics—the characteristics of a group that emerge from their beliefs, values and attitudes. To gauge reactions to a potential new HUMMER GM quizzed consumers on the entire world of SUVs. These consumer clinics, which started late in 1999 and continued through March 2000 in a string of cities, including Dallas, Chicago, Los Angeles, and Portland, pulled out insights General Motors had expected—and some they hadn't. Shown pictures of several different potential vehicles, growing increasingly aggressive and more Hummer-like, consumers responded in many different ways. "We wanted to find what turned people off, too," Hernandez says. "This wasn't going to be for everybody...but where do you draw the line?"

One consumer profile amused the people on the other side of the two-way glass in every city they visited. "They were the ones who walked in, they were probably mostly male. They sorted through the pictures, which included a couple of dummies that weren't even vehicles at all. 'Who's the company that would make this?' we'd ask. 'I know who this is. This is a Jeep. This is a Mercedes. This is a Porsche.' You're sitting behind the one-way glass, chuckling to yourself."

Some consumers were asked about General Motors' involvement in the project, and some were not. "Some thought GM would screw it up," Hernandez admits. "Others saw it as a real positive in terms of dealers, manufacturing expertise and service." Ultimately, the responses helped GM flesh out how much of itself it would inject into the public image of HUMMER and vice-versa. "Ultimately we decided, there are times it's appropriate to beat our chest and be under the GM umbrella," Hernandez says. "And other times it's just HUMMER as an entity. If we're talking about the vehicle itself, HUMMER is the place to be."

What came out in stark relief was the future HUMMER's appeal to vehicle on terms of its styling and in terms of its capability.

On those axes, its readings were off the charts of established SUV brands—the only vehicle to do so in GM's studies.

Reconciling those opposites made Hernandez and Mercer Management Consulting, a Boston-based marketing company, sift through the data and give labels to the two groups. The smaller group—the one that saw a potential new HUMMER as the ultimate off-road companion, they labeled "rugged individualists," people who often were artists, and often more attuned to the outdoors. The much larger group saw the future HUMMER's style as its linchpin—they were the "successful achievers, an affluent but hands-on group including surgeons, architects, and engineers. Whatever direction GM went with the HUMMER, it would have to combine the interests of those groups without alienating the other."

The one label that fitted both groups like an Abercrombie duster was "daring." Of the people that were taken with the HUMMER idea, the word had resonance, even with the Wall Street investment bankers and arbitrage negotiators. Psychographics, Hernandez says, explains it all. "If we filled up the room with the successful achievers and asked them, 'Why are you daring?' they'd respond, 'I just bought 200,000 shres of some dot-com stock this morning.' The risky arbitrage, the risky deal—they considered themselves daring because they make multi-million-dollar, even life and death decisions."

Even more striking was HUMMER's presence among younger consumers. "There is some 14-year-old rugged individualist out there who's dying to get a HUMMER—and at some point in his life, if things work out, and he wants a HUMMER, he's going to get it. There's some 15-year-old girl, a successful achiever, she's going to do the same thing." HUMMER is the vehicle that most people under 18 years old aspire to, and today, it's the number-one selling die cast model in the world.

Going strictly by leaning on HUMMER's military career would be wrong, everyone agreed. "It would have been easy to go down the military path," DiGiovanni says, "but it would have been a mistake."

"People die in wars," Hernandez says. "Our vehicle was instrumental in the Persian Gulf war and Operation Iraqi Freedom. Humvees performed well and their DNA is a part of us. But it's a quiet confidence, because there's going to be a day that American soldiers die in a Humvee."

Concept to reality

Translating the Humvee essence into a concept vehicle would give GM the chance to show the world it could do the brand justice. But it would also only give the company about six months to do a concept vehicle for the most important domestic auto show of all – about half the time General Motors normally would take to develop a concept.

On top of that, GM hadn't yet nailed down a deal with AM General. Though the Chunk concept had been floating around before GM even approached AM General about a partnership, the concept that was begun in the summer of 1999 wasn't shown to Armour or AM General until the fall of the year.

The decision to base the concept on GM's full-size truck/SUV platform was an easy one. It was GM's most capable vehicle closest in size to the Humvee, and was in the midst of a production rollout. The initiative to do the Humvee-inspired concept came from within GM Design, Cherry says, as was the instinct to wrap a HUMMER look around the full-size platform.

The design team moved quickly from digital models to sketches to full-size clay mock-ups. Because of the compressed timing, many steps were circumvented. "A lot of design work is done in full-size clay—what you'd like to do is more extensive full-size drawings, with time for sketches, then you go into a series of scale models to refine and choose a direction. Then you mill that shape out without much change."

From Cherry's perspective, the idea always would be for the concept to flavor a range of HUMMERs, not a lone model. A set of elements could define the HUMMER look and be easily translatable up in size—or down. "Hummers have a very specific form vocabulary, which we did an excellent job of capturing. The front end is a horizontal element bookended by round lights and square apertures, with seven slots the same height as the lighting." And what's beneath that instantly recognizable grille is just as important, Cherry says. "Right from the start, we felt that what you see underneath the vehicle is as important as the vehicle itself. It communicates the off-road capability of the vehicle…second to none."

But doing the actual concept work meant virtual secrecy within a corporation known for internal arguments, information leaks and a tendency to pre-announce news. Clay Dean was named the chief designer for the HUMMER concept and immediately began work in August in a suburban studio at Venture Industries, one of the fraternity of suppliers living in the shadow of the Big Three in southeastern Michigan. There, in a studio covered in sketches of all body styles, including pickups and a HUMMER hot rod, Dean brought the notions of HUMMER looks and GM truck chassis into fusion.

Like his parallels within the marketing side, Dean and the design team were determined not to turn HUMMER into another GM failure: "We [wanted] to make sure most of all that we don't drop the ball." The task: design a HUMMER that predicts the future of the brand, while making it consumer-friendly and capable like no other vehicle on the planet. Dean's team grabbed the challenge and, once the critical elements of positioning and platforms were decided, produced a scale model of what would become the HUMMER concept in less than a week. That vehicle emerged almost intact as the final concept. "We didn't derail from our first vision," Dean said. "All we did was enhance it. We were very confident that what we had done was correct for the vehicle."

All the while, GM sought AM General's input in the project. "Their involvement was key," Dean said. "They made sure we were true to the essence and heritage of HUMMER, and they had great insight. After they reviewed the vehicle they were confident that we were going in the right direction with the brand."

It was there that Jim Armour first saw the concept, in October of 1999 when the deal between the companies still was being detailed and had hit some sticking points. Armour's buy-in came in the form of a long walk around the concept vehicle. A quiet kind of guy, as most of the HUMMER team describes him, Armour looked at the concept in silence, finally breaking it by admitting, "There's no doubt about it in my mind. You guys have got it."

As imagined, then designed, then translated into a rolling concept vehicle, the HUMMER concept was tagged the H2—as GM planned to take the existing Hummer and rebadge it the H1. The concept sported an undeniably "Hummer" face, with a seven-slot grille and round headlamps, a winch for off-road extractions and hooks for pulling out lesser vehicles from the much. The bodysides were rounded slightly, more like a standard truck than a military-issue Humvee, with fewer bolt heads and rivets. Most unusual on the concept was a full-length canvas sunroof. And of course, the concept was intended to be built from sheet metal, not the aluminum of the original Humvee. Skid plates protected the underside of the concept (from rocky press reviews?) and the HUMMER concept sported a hybrid rear suspension not quite the independent setup of the Humvee or H1, but not a live-axle arrangement like GM's full-size pickup trucks. In fact the suspension was a five-link arrangement borrowed in part from the upcoming Chevrolet Tahoe/GMC Yukon SUVs based on the truck platform, and yet to enter production. Huge 19-inch wheels with 35-inch tires capped off the package neatly, while a version of GM's big 6.0-liter V-8 was stuffed under the hood, mated to a four-speed automatic transmission and full-time four-wheel drive. Finished off in Signal Yellow, chosen because of its association with outdoor sports equipment.

Some of the high-tech equipment integrated into the concept drew directly from the Humvee's military heritage. GPS navigation is one of the other technologies translated directly from the military to consumer use, and it was fitted to the concept vehicle, along with Night Vision from Raytheon, a military-derived system that uses infrared to detect objects ahead on the road. Internet access and laptop and cell-phone docking capability also figured into the concept. "The technology is there not to entertain as much as it is to enhance the H2's role as protector," Dean said.

GM Drops the Bomb

In the auto industry, news is a controlled substance. So when General Motors decided it was time to tell the world it had acquired the rights to sell HUMMERs, the automotive press lined up in need of a fix to follow the binge-acquisition string it had been hooked on for two years running.

GM was facing image problems, but it had the bandwidth and the bank balance to do something with the Hummer nameplate. And they were willing to strike a deal that left AM General with the family jewels intact—its lucrative military contracts. Not only that, as talks progressed, GM agreed that it would help finance a new plant on AM General's turf to build

The HUMMER H1 proves itself on the red rock trails of Moab, Utah.

the new consumer HUMMER—and that the plant would become property of AM General should the deal be allowed to expire. Best of all, AM General could dip into GM's vast parts bin to buy more up to date engines for the Hummer, like GM's 6.5-liter diesel and its more powerful V-8 gas engines.

Soon enough, Armour and GM's team of executives had locked down the terms of the deal. GM would get the rights to sell Hummer-brand vehicles for seven and a half years, while AM General would continue to build military trucks and build the new GM-derived vehicle, too. Both would survive and prosper. In August of 2000, construction began on the new plant at AM General's compound in Mishawaka; by December of 2001 HUMMER H2 pilot vehicles were rolling off the assembly line, for an on-sale date of July 2002.

Certainly AM General would benefit from the deal. GM had seemingly engineered profits without much of the risk associated with buying all of AM General. HUMMER could bring General Motors $15,000 in gross profit per vehicle, adding $500 million to the company's bottom line if it could boost volumes to 200,000 units a year. More important it could bring back customers who would never consider another GM product outside of one with the HUMMER's swagger and bravado.

"People don't appreciate how important HUMMER is to GM," GM Vice-Chairman Robert A. Lutz told *BusinessWeek*. "It's going to be a big moneymaker."

The North American International Auto Show of 2000 literally was the beginning of a new millennium in car design. "It was a big product show," Cherry says. "The year 2000 was the future—people would talk about it in books—and because of the historic importance, I wanted to show a concept for each one of our divisions." From the Tokyo motor show of 1999, where the Chevrolet

Triax was unveiled, through the Detroit show to the New York auto show in April, GM did just that, predicting the future of its divisions through concepts.

The Detroit show, however, eclipsed all. GM staged its press conference in a vast corner of Detroit's Cobo Hall in a multi-level display costing upwards of tens of millions of dollars. After running through the other divisions and closing the curtain as if the show was over, those who headed out early to grab seats at the next press conference missed the unveil of the hour—the curtains opened once more and the HUMMER H2 concept appeared in screaming-yellow. "We're going to produce an all-new HUMMER and it will look a lot like the H2," hinted Ron Zarrella, president of GM's North American automotive operations. Not only that, the vehicle would be in production within two years, he said—astonishing timing for the company generally reputed as the slowest to steer in Detroit.

The H2 concept fought for attention, but in a hail of new concepts and new products that included a slinky F-Type from Jaguar, the Chevrolet Avalanche, the new MINI Cooper from BMW, and the Norwegian-bred eco-TH!NK car from Ford, the HUMMER got its due as one of the most important concepts on the floor that day—in GM's words, "an authentic evolution in a truly incomparable species."

GM's timing couldn't have been more dramatic. HUMMER designers worked on concepts at home to avoid detection of the deal before the concept made its debut, mating HUMMER proportions to a Chevy Tahoe chassis and literally taping their ideas together as the stage lights were lit in Detroit on January 9, 2000—the first auto show of the new millennium. GM and AM General took HUMMER off into more uncharted territory as the H2 Vision concept took the stage. Cameras clicked and journalists did too, in murmured approval as Zarrella promised the world a new HUMMER.

The announcement of the deal neatly capped the wave of consolidation just about to draw to a close in Detroit. All the good brands had been snapped up, and when GM announced the deal in early 2000, it met with low whistles of approval, for the bravado of buying into an unestablished but gold-star brand and by unveiling its H2 Vision concept, maybe the butchest looking truck at that year's Detroit auto show. GM framed the deal as a win-win for it and AM General—and then sat down to the business of putting HUMMER to work.

Chapter 7

H2: Stinger Missiles and Soccer Moms

"You give us the money, we give you the truck. Nobody gets hurt."—**Advertisement for the HUMMER H2**

General Motors and AM General had caught the attention of the world with the unveiling the HUMMER H2 Vision concept in Detroit. The most capable SUVs on the planet were about to become the brand that would take over the world, literally and figuratively, in the space of a few years, boosting both companies' fortunes and drawing the arrows of the anti-SUV crowd in their direction.

No less an authority than Bob Lutz thought the idea was "a genuine stroke of genius." Lutz, a longtime auto exec admired for his sense of product, is seen as one of the caretakers of Detroit's car sensibilities. Lutz had worked at Chrysler during its darkest days, as part of the management team that avoided bankruptcy in 1991 and reinvigorated the company with a new range of vehicles, from the class-leading Grand Caravan minivan to the exotic, $75,000 two-seat Viper, thundering along behind the power of a massive V-10 engine. So strong was Lutz's reputation that GM CEO Rick Wagoner sought him out in August 2000, hiring him to come in as vice chairman of product development to clear the cobwebs from the company's notoriously laborious product development.

Car guy Lutz, also a cigar aficionado, helicopter pilot and former Navy man, was taken by the HUMMER concept and by the ballsy show at Detroit. "I've been really captivated by who had the idea," Lutz says while explaining the finer points of GM's new Pontiac GTO, the Corvette-powered successor to the Sixties musclecar at an event in California in 2003. "I've obviously heard several versions, depending on who you talk to," he says.

"Frankly we had the idea at Chrysler of the vehicle, but it never occurred to us to go to AM General, which would have been logical because AM General and Jeep used to be the same company. They even have the same grille," he muses.

"I knew GM was going to do it when I saw the yellow concept vehicle at the Detroit auto show. I thought to myself, boy, this is going to be really bad news, because if GM does this right, this could become the next big thing in sport-utility vehicles."

Lutz wasn't alone in believing the HUMMER brand had vast potential for GM. Within the companies themselves, a sense of pride in the project took over. Engineers recruited to turn the concept vehicle into reality volunteered for the task, and families living near the AM General factory moved to accommodate the new plant needed to build the vehicle.

From all around, the time pressures were enormous. GM and AM General would build their first vehicle in December 2001, only 16 months from turning over the first shovel of dirt on Chippewa Avenue. Coming from a company too tiny to expand by itself, and from a company that hadn't replaced its entry-level sedan the Cavalier since 1984, the timeline was aggressive, tricky, even dangerous—and ultimately the driving force behind its lightning success.

Concept to reality

But before AM General could build the first H2, plenty of work had to be done in GM's halls of development. While GM and AM General worked on finishing off the contract in the summer and fall of 1999, and began their noodlings from a concept car based on existing GM parts, translating the concept into reality from its hybrid chassis would be a crash course in engineering on a small scale from GM's vast parts bin.

The approach to the design of the concept had given the production engineering team a major leg up in putting the H2 into showrooms. The objective didn't need to be stated: everyone involved wanted to build the concept as is. "The objective for everyone was how to do that vehicle," says Cherry. "A lot of intense effort went into bringing that vehicle into production," as opposed to a more easily manufactured vehicle bearing a resemblance to the concept.

Ken Lindensmith was the engineer in charge of taking the baton from the concept team and developing what would become the final H2. Like many within GM, he thought the idea of the HUMMER brand had some merit, that it might be a home run. Around Easter of 1999, while Lindensmith worked with others to seal the AM General deal, he realized it was going to work—as did his wife. "You guys are absolutely nuts,'" he recalls her saying. Until Lindensmith brought home a prototype and drove it to their lake home in Irish

HUMMER

Hills, she remained unconvinced. "We got stopped like 30 times, people wanting to come out and talk, people we'd never seen before."

He recalls that much of the conceptual work was done early on in negotiations with AM General. "We had a debriefing session [after the MOI was signed], and started to develop what the H2 would become: off the sport-utilities, the 3/4-ton version. We'd have to upgrade the suspension. The gas engine would be sufficient—our 6.0-liter engine was a pretty good performer. We studied the diesel as well, but threw it out—it would have meant extending the vehicle another 6 to 8 inches for the cooling package. It wouldn't look like a HUMMER," he says.

By September of that year, Lindensmith was named project manager for the HUMMER vehicle and started to put together a vehicle development team. Though the project still didn't have official approval—it would go to the board of directors in late November—it was "too big of an idea to get scuttled."

The approval came in December, nearly a rubber stamp to a project moving so fast, it required lightning decisions just to keep the project on track. "We got a loan approved, all the funds approved for tooling, and approval to get additional engineering monies."

By December, when the project had been approved, Lindensmith was able to add about ten General Motors employees to his ranks. That supplied him with the lead engineering to guide the project—but GM didn't have enough product engineers to spare for the H2. "This was not a vehicle program GM had at all in its portfolio plan," he says. The solution was to hire contract engineers from EDAG, a company that had done some work on the Saturn L-Series, in January 2000. EDAG in turn hired Ricardo, Britain's racing firm, to develop the chassis and suspension for GM. Between GM's lead engineers and the contracted help, the core of the H2 engineering team was in place.

H2: Stinger Missiles and Soccer Moms

GM dealers who want to sell the HUMMER brand must build stand-alone dealerships with design cues from military buildings.

Still, the final shape of the H2 was not locked in, though the vehicle would end up being remarkably faithful to the concept shown in Detroit. For a final call, HUMMER held a design contest within the company to tweak the final shape of the H2. Two internal studios at GM's tech center in Warren, Mich., competed, as did GM's design studio on the west coast, in suburban Los Angeles. On a Saturday morning early in 2000, the HUMMER team viewed the competing concepts at the GM styling dome in Detroit. One version was essentially the concept vehicle, with changes to accommodate what could be possible in production. "The other two had a couple of good ideas," Lindensmith offers, "but we had gotten so much feedback on the concept, we thought we can make the vehicle look pretty much like that. This was a program where the engineers wanted to produce that exact vehicle. They came to the program saying, 'I want to figure out how to build that vehicle.'"

In February, the HUMMER team began to make a real vehicle from the concept's guidelines. But the original concept had done some things that couldn't be brought to bear quickly enough. The concept had an independent suspension like that on the original Humvee. And it had done so in a clever way: "Clay [Dean] used front suspension components [from GM's forthcoming full-size SUVs], flipped them and put them on the rear. The timing...didn't fit with the plan we had," Lindensmith says. And when GM asked Hummer owners about it, "they said it's gotta have an independent suspension," which allows the original Humvee to articulate over obstacles better. Eventually, the HUMMER team settled on a five-link suspension that would endow the H2 with good off-road clearance and wheel articulation and durability, while not truly mimicking the original Hummer. The front suspension would be derived from GM's 3/4-ton pickup trucks, while the rear suspension would be borrowed from the half-ton models—all parts available

H2: Stinger Missiles and Soccer Moms

through GM's existing suppliers without modification, a critical engineering short-cut that helped speed up the development process.

As the team began evaluating the vehicle—to ensure it delivered as much ground-covering capability as possible to fit in the HUMMER brand—it became clear the team would spend a lot of time off-roading. The whole subject of true off-roading in terms of SUVs is a controversial one. For years, many makers have operated under the assumption that less than five percent of SUV customers actually drive their vehicles in an off-road environment—not gravel or dusty roads, but off the mapped byways and into true off-road territory, where fallen trees can end a trip as surely as a flat tire, if the vehicle doesn't have the right amount of ground clearance. Some makers, such as Land Rover and Jeep, rightly figure their owners do venture into more off-roading than is usual, particularly with Jeep and second and third owners of its inexpensive Wranglers. Still for the vast majority of SUV buyers—those who own Ford Escapes, Honda Pilots and Chevrolet Trackers—the rule is the road, not the less beaten path.

HUMMER's reputation lies almost entirely in off-road excursions, though, whether in the blinding sands of Kuwait or the swampy muck of Panama. So off-road capability being a piece of HUMMER "DNA," the team devoted much more energy to off-road development they ever assumed they would. "The original drive had told us we had to do more in body protection work. And throughout the development process, AM General served as a really good conscience for us."

To ensure the H2 could meet the most difficult off-road challenges, the HUMMER team took prototypes to the major off-road venues known and loved by enthusiasts—the slick rock trails of Moab, Utah, muddy mountain passes in Tellico, N.C., and the ultimate off-road challenge, California's Rubicon Trail. Through these off-roading trips, HUMMER engineers worked out the traction-control system for the vehicle, adding a button to allow experienced drivers to override some of its use at low speeds—because in snow and in mud, a little slip can give the traction needed to get out of a rut. HUMMER also sought out some expert advice from off-road racing champion Rod Hall to develop the vehicle's suspension and off-road characteristics.

The HUMMER team also wanted some input from another critical audience it had to woo even before the first vehicles were delivered. Automotive journalists might be swayed by the truck's looks, but the subset of off-road writers would need more convincing. HUMMER did something out of character by bringing in the off-road books in the summer of 2001, allowing the journalists to drive prototypes and give suggestions about the vehicles before the production started. The media drove the trucks across the Rubicon Trail, with nose bras on the trucks to blur their identity somewhat. "We were nervous—we took untested trucks across the Rubicon," Lindensmith says. Aside from small interior issues, the group came away impressed.

Any auto exec will tell you development work is never complete. Even when production vehicles begin to drive off the end of an assembly line, minor details are changed constantly, either to improve appearance or functionality or to make the vehicle cheaper and easier to build. Many vehicles improve in reliability over their lifetime because better ways to build them with fewer moving parts are implemented. But a lock-off point comes when a vehicle is handed off to the factory with no changes made for a few months, while production ramps up and engineers figure out if the plant is building things properly and how to build it better.

Up to the last minute, Lindensmith's engineers were scrambling to finish work on the H2. The concept for the interior had morphed along the way. "We started with the concept that it might be a hose-out interior," he says. "All the luxury was in the underpinnings, was the thinking. We didn't mean it to be a luxury vehicle, but more a prestige vehicle." But continual marketing research kept indicating buyers perceived the vehicle as a luxury item. The interior was the biggest disappointment to the team. "It still falls short of where we would like it to be," he says.

But just two years after GM and AM General had signed off on the deal that would create the H2, the companies had built a brand-new plant next to the assembly line that puts together TOW-missile Humvees and begun building the first HUMMERs truly designed for civilian use. A brief timeline shows how quickly General Motors—always perceived as the leviathan among Detroit's automakers—and AM General had moved in order to get the program going. In early 1999, the companies first met to discuss the idea of jointly developing and selling HUMMERs. In December 1999 the contract was finalized.

In early 2000, AM General had convinced owners of 51 homes next to the proposed H2 plant to sell their homes so the company could build more parking and delivery space for the new vehicles. The homes, known as "area 51" to the company, couldn't be bought out expensively: "We simply didn't have the cash," CEO Armour said. Over the next eight months the company bought all 51 homes and had 47 owners return for a special tour and dedication of the 630,000-square-foot plant. No eminent domain helped them along—just the goodwill of the community eager to grow more jobs in their backyard.

By September of 2000, engineers had locked in the shape of some of the first sheetmetal panels that would make up the final vehicle. And by December 21, 2001, AM General built the first running vehicles at the plant. "The way we measure programs as an industry, we talk about 24-month programs or 18-month programs, which is what GM wants to get to," Lindensmith says. For the HUMMER H2, measuring from when the last major sheetmetal panel was designed to first saleable vehicle, "we actually did it in 15 months."

Arnold buys in

The H2 had proved its mettle off road, to GM's team and AM General's as well as a core of influential journalists. Families were willing to give up their homes to make HUMMER a household icon. But one piece of the puzzle in GM's marketing plan was obvious, and obviously missing—and negotiating the relationship with the then-future governor of California to join the HUMMER team would be as difficult to engineer and as essential as the H2's off-road capability.

Arnold Schwarzenegger had been the ambassador for HUMMER longer than the brand had civilian customers. It was his thick Austrian accent, only somewhat tempered by three decades in America, and his leather-clad Terminator persona that was associated directly with the Humvee first, then the civilian Hummer.

So universal was Arnold's connection with Hummer that, from the summer negotiations between AM General and General Motors, bringing Arnold on board had been an issue with the HUMMER team. HUMMER team members were big fans of Arnold Schwarzenegger. But AM General's relationship with the governor of California had always been one of friendship: no money changed hands, and Arnold was more an ambassador for the brand than a commercial spokesman. GM's team saw the stardust scattered over the Humvee, and even before formally linking with Schwarzenegger, used him as inspiration.

"I went to see *Terminator* three times," DiGiovanni admits. "I'd like to see *T4*, frankly." It was DiGiovanni's idea, "dammit," that the project stay underground—and the best way to keep it a secret within GM was to give it a code name: "Project Maria," after Arnold's wife, Maria Shriver.

"I came up with that – no matter who says that, it was my name," DiGiovanni adamantly says. "We hadn't even had any relationship at that point," he adds, "but every piece of product research we did, Arnold's name came up. We need a code name for this, because everybody was sniffing around from the outside."

By the fall of 1999, Schwarzenegger had begun to show interest in GM's upcoming HUMMER project, which had barely been alluded to in the press. DiGiovanni banked on Arnold's interest growing when he saw what GM had prepared so far, so in November of 1999, AM General CEO Jim Armour and Arnold paid a visit to GM's styling studio, where the H2 mockup was in progress.

"So this is Maria, the beast," he quipped.

"He was pretty excited when he saw the vehicle," recalls GM design chief Cherry. "From the first time, he was very enthusiastic." So enthusiastic that he offered critiques on what the HUMMER should be and what it should have—maybe some jump seat in the back for kids, possibly a thicker A-pillar and a more upright windshield. But his overall impression was similar to Armour's: GM had done right by the HUMMER name.

GM would continue to keep Schwarzenegger in the design loop throughout its process, from unveiling the concept vehicle in Detroit through the translation into a real consumer vehicle, running pictures out for him to see as design mockups grew closer to production reality. But until after the concept was shown to the public, GM had no official deal with the Terminator on any level other than a hearty approval.

"After the Detroit show and the H2 concept vehicle, Arnold's agents started calling me," DiGiovanni recalls. "He was interested in

HUMMER

A star is born.

exploring a relationship with HUMMER because he created the brand and he wanted to be a part of it. The problem was he wanted a *lot* of money. The numbers were staggering at the beginning," DiGiovanni recalls.

"I told his agent, I have to pay for this out of my budget, [out of] marketing funds used to promote the brand. I said I'd love to but I can't do it. I called off negotiations."

DiGiovanni's plan to get Arnold in on the concept-car reveal in Detroit hadn't worked—and now a crucial linchpin in the brand's history was off the market. "Zarrella told me, 'You blew it, you made a mistake,'" DiGiovanni says.

But despite the loggerheads, both sides still wanted to complete a deal. They resumed talks around Easter 2000, when Arnold's agents called DiGiovanni with a new approach from Schwarzenegger himself. "'Arnold has come up with an idea,'" DiGiovanni recalls the approach. "The money would go to sponsor what was then called the Inner City Games, and would be a charitable donation, which would give us both a whole world of benefits."

Schwarzenegger's Inner City Games, begun in 1991 in Los Angeles and now established in 15 cities, helps those cities establish programs to offer teens sports and computer-education activities during summer and afterschool hours—what the foundation calls "critical hours" when drug use violence and teen pregnancy occur most often. A nonprofit organization, the Inner City Games Foundation is chaired by Schwarzenegger and has spawned a similar program for middle-school students, Arnold's All Stars. In 2003 the foundation renamed its program the After-School All-Stars.

"Most stars would just write a check," DiGiovanni explains. "He goes to Detroit, Philadelphia, to schools in the inner city, he speaks to these kids, and tells them, 'You can be a winner in life.' These kids look at him like a god. How many people of his stature do that? It's unreal."

"It was a tough negotiation," DiGiovanni recalls. "His agent said he felt it was the toughest negotiation he'd ever done." In the end, DiGiovanni says that GM donated $13 million to the foundation in return for Arnold making appearances on behalf of HUMMER.

The deal had an unintentional bonus for one dad's street cred. DiGiovanni's own kids didn't believe that Arnold was involved in it, until the afternoon the actor left a message on DiGiovanni's home phone. His children heard it – and asked the neighborhood kids in to gloat over it.

"We embraced Arnold Schwarzenegger from day one," he says. "If Arnold didn't like the H2, if it wasn't an authentic HUMMER, I don't think we would have been nearly as successful. He was part of the family.

General Motors might have spent millions in clever ads to launch its HUMMER vehicles, and two decades of military experience may have forged its reputation. But the veneer of celebrity that comes with every H1 or H2 couldn't have happened without the attraction of the last action hero. And getting his buy-in removed the last major source of doubt GM had when it came to building its own HUMMER—the star factor was secured. If they hadn't had it, Arnold could have dismissed the project with an offhand comment.

Or as DiGiovanni says thankfully, "What if he had said, 'That's girly?'"

Selling the vision

Beyond production of the vehicle and Arnold's blessing, General Motors looked to the public to make sure its gamble on the H2 project would pay off. Marketing study after marketing study

H2: Stinger Missiles and Soccer Moms

indicated a big hit, even priced just south of $50,000. But exactly how to appeal to those customers came to marketing—and like the original Humvee, GM took its battle everywhere with sheer presence.

The first move GM made was to cherry-pick advertising talent in the shape of Harvard MBA Liz Vanzura, who had made a reputation for innovation by commissioning a series of Volkswagen ads that paired modern music, poetic ad copy and arresting images in both print and television. A former GM brand exec who worked on the unexciting Pontiac Sunfire, Vanzura had been director of advertising and marketing for Volkswagen from 1996 to 2000. Vanzura joined the HUMMER team on March 1, 2001, roughly the same time DiGiovanni had brought on Modernista!, a small New England agency whose principals had worked with Vanzura at VW to craft ads for the revived New Beetle, among other new vehicles.

When HUMMER recruited Vanzura to develop their SUV advertising, she was intent on making it look different from the stock and trade of other SUV ads. "Every single one of them looked the same," she recalls. "Every SUV was crossing boulders. You couldn't tell the difference between them."

HUMMER's demographic target—30-44 year olds with incomes of more than $150,000—gave Vanzura license for some exciting advertising, she says. Fully a quarter of them would be women, so any campaign would have to appeal to them strongly. Market research showed that the H2 appealed to women—one dealer, in fact, told Vanzura that the women who did buy HUMMERs were women "who didn't need permission to buy them," while many of the men were men who did.

Advertising for the new H2 launched in the summer of 2001, months before the vehicle would be ready for sale. The first campaign used a yellow H2 against a blue-sky landscape with the tagline, "Like

167

nothing else." Ad lines were targeted by publications: the sophisticated metrosexual audience of *Vanity Fair*, for example, got "Threaten the men in your office in a whole new way," while *Forbes* gets, "You give us the money, we give you the truck. Nobody gets hurt."

Vanzura's favorite, though, is "Big Time," in which a boy gets a note which says cryptically, *first one down wins*. The challenge is for a soapbox derby—and the boy builds the winning vehicle, an H2 lookalike, and wins by running it across the racetrack, through mud and rocks.

But advertising is far from the only means in building awareness. HUMMER's concept for publicity took it to every nook of awareness, from a Web presence to the toys children play with. The model was, in fact, more like a movie launch: action figures and die cast models already in place, the HUMMER made its way into the first season of CBS' *CSI: Miami* and other television shows. A dedicated Web site selling HUMMER gear, www.hummerstuff.com, was established to deal with the hundreds of thousands of customers who weren't ready to plunk down $50,000 for the H2, but could swing a $15 hat.

And Vanzura broke new ground by commissioning a video with the H2 from producers Timbaland and Ms. Jade to feature the H2, the video called "Ching Ching Ching." Timbaland, the hip-hop producer who fueled Missy Elliott's "Get Ur Freak On," crafted a hit that brought the H2 the kind of street cred Cadillac had unexpectedly earned with the knife-edged Escalade. HUMMER released the video to MTV, where it rose as high as number eight on the network's daily *Total Request Live* countdown show.

Equal parts vehicle and marketing "big bang," the Hummer H2 is almost without parallel in the auto industry in concept, timing, execution, efficiency and bang for GM's buck. BMW's micro MINI brand would come shortly thereafter and would set the example for

H2: Stinger Missiles and Soccer Moms

The signature big-block HUMMER logo is instantly recognizable, on the streets or in the wild.

selling low-priced goods as high fashion, but it was HUMMER that proved a huge SUV with Army roots could be sold like fine art.

Reception and reviews

A final piece of the launch puzzle was in lining up positive reviews by automotive journalists and analysts. The way car companies do this is through "long-lead" press events catering to publications that take more time to go to press—like monthly magazines—and "short-lead" events that include all types of outlets from Web sites to daily newspapers to the marketing analysts from investment firms and groups like J.D. Power and Associates.

These events can be barebone introductions conducted out of a local restaurant for nearby journalists—or can brave the luxurious territory of first-class events, with stays at posh resorts like the Sanctuary in Paradise Valley, Ariz., the Ritz-Carlton at Half Moon Bay on the California coast, or even international destinations like the jungles of Belize or the moors of Scotland and Skibo Castle.

The HUMMER H2 drive took place at the birthplace of the military Humvee in South Bend, Ind. HUMMER knew that its credibility was at stake with a whole new audience, and what better place to prove it out than the place it hailed from? The opinions that would be printed in millions of papers and seen on hours of TV coverage would be almost uniformly great for the HUMMER team.

"It's the perfect urban assault vehicle, missing only a gun turret and its own U.N. inspection team" was one sentiment typical of reviews of the H2 when the production version finally showed its face in 2002. J.D. Power and Associates analyst Jeffrey Schuster called the move for GM to take the HUMMER brand rights "brilliant."

The most respected car magazines checked in with praise for the HUMMER H2, as well. "The H2 may not be able to climb a three-foot wall, traverse a 40-percent slope, or straddle a 16-inch boulder, as the H1 can. But it is clearly equipped to be the most capable GM-designed off-roader on the market. It has the strike-force styling of the now-legendary AM General Humvee and its civilian clone the Hummer, though it's much more refined. And starting at about $49,000, the H2 costs less than half the original's price," said *Car and Driver* in January 2003.

And in another review, C/D's Tony Swan said the HUMMER had the capability to transform its pilots: "A mysterious metamorphosis occurs during the climb into the cockpit of this most militant of all Tahoe/Suburbans. The driver begins experiencing Mittyesque visions of El Alamein and Desert Storm. What we have here is a shameless appeal to latent male adolescence, with exterior styling that cries out for camo paint and machine-gun mounts. Although far more civilized than the original H1, it has few other redeeming virtues, aside from plentiful ground clearance. The love of my life called it 'the male equivalent of a push-up bra,' and I find it hard to argue otherwise. But in the secret depths of my psyche, ruled by my inner 12-year-old, I *love* this thing."

More mainstream press even approved of the H2's outrageous exterior and extreme off-road capability, though not many owners would ever tax it. "Those rough looks probably will sell all 30,000 or so H2s a year that GM plans," wrote Jim Healey in *USA Today*. "Assuming you're not so addicted to one-upmanship that you've long had an H1, then H2 will be your vision of the ultimate SUV: rugged enough for near-military duty, refined enough for soccer- parent errands."

Behind the wheel

Probably the most intimidating vehicle on the road today, the HUMMER H2 is surprisingly docile on the road. But as might be expected, it's a mountain goat in the muck, able to claw its way over rocks and trees and pull out of mud pits that aren't too prevalent in Kroger parking lots but can be conquered on a long weekend drive.

Based on the Tahoe/Suburban platform but shortened and reinforced heavily for more demanding off-road use, the H2 sports a 122.8-inch wheelbase and an overall body length of 189.8 inches. The H2 is 7.3 inches shorter and 4.9 inches narrower than the imposing H1. In other words, it will fit into normal parking spaces even better than Chevy's Tahoe and the HUMMER H1.

Beneath the sheetmetal the H2 owes its front control-arm and torsion-bar suspension to the 2500-series Suburban as well as its live-axle, air-spring, five-link setup in the rear. Retuned for off-road driving, the H2 also wears monotube shocks on all four corners for superior ride control.

The size and shape make it much more maneuverable around town than the bigger Humvee-based H1. But the H2 retains much of the H1's off-road prowess. It can crash through six inches of water at 40 mph, tug its way slowly through 20-inch-deep water, and clamber over a 16-inch tall wall or step. You may not want to dent its Tonka-toy body panels on the rocks, but the H2 will go as far as most off-road vehicles (save for dense woods where it can't actually fit between the trees).

The H2's powertrain is far more suited for the open road than that on the H1. It's a 6.0-liter GM V-8, with 315 horsepower and 360 pound-feet of torque, coupled to a four-speed automatic transmission. This is GM's stock truck powertrain, and a smooth, powerful combination in every package it's used in, from the H2 to the Silverado pickup to the Cadillac Escalade. Because it's hauling heavy-duty weight, the H2 accelerates far more quickly than the H1, but it'll have trouble dusting a hybrid Toyota Prius since it takes a little more than 10 seconds to cruise to 60 mph. And because it

H2: Stinger Missiles and Soccer Moms

Full-time four-wheel drive on every H2 means lots of traction, even when the dirt goes flying.

weighs about 6400 pounds, the H2 evades any kind of fuel-economy regulations, though GM admits that in normal circumstances 13 mpg is a stretch for the massive SUV.

The H2's trail-carving ability comes from its four-wheel-drive system, a full-time setup that uses a BorgWarner transfer case and center differential to split the engine's power evenly between the front and rear wheels when needed. But if that's not sufficient, H2 buyers can order special all-terrain tires and more protection for the underbody of the vehicle.

Inside the interior space isn't all that great, but five can fit reasonably well. HUMMER execs say the interior is the feature they'd most like to have spent more time and money on. It's certainly less exotic than GM's own Caddy Escalade interior, and the grade of plastics doesn't seem to fit the mission of a $50,000 vehicle. GM says upgrades in the interior trim are on the way.

But the minor quibbles hardly seem important when you strap on the H2. Like the Humvee and Hummer before it, the H2 isn't so much a serious vehicle as it is a mobile fantasy. Hop in the driver's seat and you can become Arnold Schwarzenegger's Terminator, G.I. Joe, or any adventure action figure you want—without having to deal with the compromises of price, visibility and comfort that the H1 imposes. As a sport-utility vehicle, the H2 is satisfactory, more capable than it is useful; as a hardcore off-road machine it's useful so long as you're willing to ignore the creases, dings and scrapes sure to come with its width.

As a dream machine, it's without a truck equal. It has no peers. Like the ads say, it's "like nothing else."

Master of its universe

Between the press drives, final engineering work, and multimedia hoopla gathering around the HUMMER H2, more work

H2: Stinger Missiles and Soccer Moms

remained on all fronts. For one, HUMMER engineers planned the first spin-off model of the GM-designed ute—a sort of half-SUV, half-truck dubbed the H2 SUT (for "sport-utility truck") that substituted a short pickup bed and a flexible tailgate and midgate for the enclosed cargo area of the H2 SUV.

To introduce it, GM cashed in a chit with Schwarzenegger and used him in an appearance staged prior to the New York Auto Show. On April 16, 2001, Arnold and then-Mayor Rudy Giuliani drove the new H2 SUT concept through Times Square, stopping traffic as they dismounted in front of ABC's New York studios and introduced the vehicle on *Good Morning America.* Not only was it Arnold's first major appearance with the HUMMER squad for the international press – it was the first time he divulged his role in the process that created the vehicle. "I was involved every step of the way," he said. Showing off the vehicle, Giuliani was understated while Arnold was all enthusiast and cheerleader: "Look at those deltoids! Look at those pecs!" he exclaimed, referring to the SUT concept.

Of course, General Motors and AM General recognized that Arnold should be one of the first owners of the H2, too. So when the companies began building the H2 in production, they brought Schwarzenegger to South Bend on the occasion of his 55th birthday and presented him with one of the first H2s, a brand-new pewter vehicle—and in kind, he endorsed the H2 as the worthy successor to the H1's legacy. "It keeps the true spirit of the Hummer for the soccer mom, for the executive, for the studly guys, for the fat guys, for the skinny guys," Schwarzenegger said. "Everyone can have a Hummer now."

By the fall, General Motors had nearly every base covered—in a way no product or brand in its lineup had jelled in decades. But troubling signs that the launch would not go perfectly were brewing, as early as the beginning of 2000, just after GM struck the official deal with AM General. For starters, the economic downturn that began discreetly in the first quarter of 2000 had picked up steam. The dot-com boom that had lifted the tide for hundreds of stocks was washing out; jobs were being lost and, as later GDP estimates would be revised, the economy actually contracted in the first quarter of 2001, months before the actual recession that gripped the country in most of 2001 took hold. Newer estimates say the recession may even have been underway with President Clinton still in office. As jobs evaporated, potential HUMMER customers were drifting out of the market and out of the picture—and the protracted worrying over the conclusion of Election 2000 didn't help the economy's stability.

Then, the lawsuits began. The HUMMER's arresting shape drew attention—not only from buyers but from DaimlerChrysler. In one of those convoluted lawsuits that could happen only in America, DaimlerChrysler sued GM over the fact that the H2's seven-bar grille looked something like Jeep's own products. Never mind the fact that both Jeep and AM General had used the grilles throughout their history—a truth a series of judges upheld in 2001 and 2002. The companies were cousins, the resemblance familial and, as was ruled, entirely legal.

Worse, there were indications that one of GM's concerns regarding environmentalists were coming true. The H2 had perfectly captured the essence of HUMMER while domesticating it for daily-driver use. It also sharply focused attention from a growing group of Americans unhappy with the growth of SUVs on the road. The problem had been magnified by the booming growth in SUV sales, and by the migration into ever-larger sport-utes. The H2's sidestep of fuel-economy regulations was seized by the Sierra Club and green activists looking to throttle a new neck, now that Ford's Excursion SUV had ceased to draw the public's interests.

And then, on September 11, 2001, the "perfect storm" came together in a terrifying day for America. While New York woke to a stunning day, an armada of hijackers were boarding planes in small airports on the East Coast, feeding into larger flights from Boston and Washington, D.C., headed for West Coast destinations. As New York and Washington began the work day, the hijackers turned the airplanes into airborne bombs, using a smattering of crude training to steer four renegade planes into four separate targets—each of the twin World Trade Center towers in New York, into the Pentagon outside Washington, D.C., and it is thought, toward the White House. Three of the planes found their targets, killing 2,982 people in and around the World Trade Center, including 300 policemen and firefighters; another 198 at the nerve center of the American military; and another 47 innocents in a field near Shanksville, Pennsylvania, who it is presumed had a role in bringing their plane down short of its target of the White House.

In the span of less than two hours, terrorists had inflicted physical and psychological damage America had not experienced in generations. It was America's new Pearl Harbor: the thundering, murderous prelude to a "war on terror." The Sept. 11 attacks killed thousands of citizens, punched a hole in America's shroud of invincibility, and spiked any hope that the languid economy would revive itself anytime soon.

September 11 ended decades of peace in America, and President George W. Bush was determined to settle the score. The military Humvee was headed back to war. For the U.S., the Humvee and its civilian cousin, the world had indeed changed. It had become less certain, more nervous, and decidedly darker.

Chapter 8

Anti-SUV Hysteria, or Arianna Takes On the H2

>Your wallet's fat, your car is rank
>F★★★ you and your H2!
>Each burst of speed costs half a tank
>F★★★ you and your H2!
>At each stop sign and traffic light
>Regardless if it's day or night
>They'll mutter "a★★hole" and they're right
>F★★★ you and your H2!

—from www.FuH2.com, a satiric Web site

SUVs aren't the perfect vehicles for every driver. For those who need them, they offer better towing, more cargo room, and off-road capability not available in a passenger car. And for every SUV buyer that truly needs off-road capability and a wagon body, 10 seem to need only a readjustment in their cranium and the keys to a Toyota Corolla.

For every overdone fad rises an equally overzealous reaction. And in the case of the SUV boom of the 1990s, the resulting anti-SUV hysteria of the early 2000s proved to be inane, poorly argued and, ultimately, used violence to substitute for logic and reason.

Witness one of the less anarchic reactions to SUV mania: John Taguiri, a 48-year-old artist from Cambridge, Mass., began issuing tickets around metro Boston for "Violation: Earth," morphing a city traffic ticket into a screed that scolded SUV buyers for wasting oil and taping the tickets to the rear windows of the vehicles. Taguiri also posted a Web site, www.earthonempty.com, where others could print and post citations on vehicles in their cities. Taguiri claims that more than a million SUVs have been tagged, in 500 cities in 48 states.

For reasons of safety, economic drag, military engagement and spiritual well-being, Americans were being exhorted to give up their bad SUV habit like some sort of four-wheel crystal meth. Only no one was getting skinny and losing their teeth from driving a Chevy Suburban. But the opponents would coalesce around a few arguments that SUVs led to terrorism and killed other innocent drivers.

No vehicle has polarized Americans like the SUV—and the HUMMER vehicles would become the poster children for SUV excess. Sport-utility vehicles had been under attack before, but the arrival of the H2 was like a sports whistle that began a free-for-all that engulfed green activists on the left, HUMMER owners on the right, and more consumers stuck in the middle, either angry at being told how stupid their admiration for HUMMERs were, or wooed by specious arguments that driving SUVs contributed to terrorism.

But the reunion of the pro-SUV titans and anti-SUV crowd hadn't merely reconstituted itself anew from the Ford "Valdez" days of 1999–it had been grown into an ongoing hate-hate relationship since then. Of the events that spurred anti-SUV hysteria between the late 1990s and the advent of the HUMMER, the accelerant likely was the the Firestone tire recall of 2000, in which a hundred-year relationship between the interrelated Ford and Firestone families was severed and 271 people died in accidents.

The list of those taking sides ranged from everyone involved in making the HUMMER to the Sierra Club, from a reverend seeking to find "what would Jesus drive?" to an SUV advocate bound to figure out instead what "Jésus" would drive, to the head of the National Highway Traffic Safety Administration and an influential journalist out to cast himself as a modern-day Nader, finally to a pair of candidates in a campaign that would ultimately end in the recall of the governor of California–with one of them crowned the winner.

In less than 15 years SUVs had grown from a few fairly primitive models to more than 50 offerings from automakers as diverse as GM and Daewoo. But the capture of HUMMER by General Motors was the tipping point into the anti-SUV hysteria, a movement that would ride the coattails of the biggest automotive recall ever, and would be psychologically linked to a presidential election that already had split the country almost precisely in half, in ideological ways that closely mirrored the split in SUV sensibilities.

Within a span of 18 months, the HUMMER had gone from a patriotic icon to a brand flagged as the epitome of American overindulgence, fueling terror as it fueled up and an elitist tool used to kill "the less fortunate." Anti-SUV zealots smelled blood with the

H2—and it was only a short time before they looked to anarchy as a solution to the HUMMER "problem."

Might is right, left is right

The ideological rift between HUMMER haters and HUMMER lovers laid itself bare in the media almost immediately after General Motors pumped new life into the glittering but underdeveloped brand.

The reckoning of one of America's most influential "car guys" chalks it up to a classic split between the doers and thinkers among America's elite. GM's Vice Chairman of product development, Bob Lutz, is himself a poster child for the good-old-boys' network that rules Detroit with a cigar-occupied hand. A white-haired patrician who's helmed major operations at each of the big American car companies, Lutz draws a fine point to the difference between HUMMER owners and fans and those who'd sooner see the vehicles blown up unmanned on the battlefield.

"The brand you drive, or the model, tends to be an expression of your own personality," Lutz says during the introduction of the 2004 Pontiac GTO, a 350-hp two-door that barely nods to practicality on its way to 60-mph runs of less than 5.3 seconds. "It's closely allied to your overall social and political views," he explains. "If you are a fairly strong left-leaning Democrat, pro-environmental, U.S. out of Nicaragua, Students for a Democratic Society, a draft avoider, or espouse anti-war causes, you're going to hate the thing because you hate rich people, you have power, and you hate the U.S. military overseas.

"It's one more manifestation of the age-old class warfare," he adds. "Not the upper and the lower, but the two educated classes. Like every country, we have two educated classes; the class that does things, creates wealth, defends the nation. The other—actors,

Articulation: not just a way of speaking, but a way of getting around sharp rocks and craggy boulders.

tourists, writers, university professors—it's not the productive educated class. Throughout history, the intellectual class has hated the productive educated class and their toys."

And in the other corner are the environmentalists and everyday drivers who've come to detest SUVs in general and the HUMMERs in specific.

A critique of the phenomenon on TheCarConnection.com, an industry news and car-review Web site, takes the opposition's case: "Most people look upon HUMMER buyers as assholes. HUMMER owners...make Corvette owners seem well adjusted and confident. HUMMER owners like Rolex watches, mink coats, Aspen skiing and multiple homes—not exactly likeable folks. HUMMERS are hated, as are HUMMER owners by the masses. HUMMER is the poster child for green-thinking people who hate big SUVs and think they are mostly a blight on the roadscape."

Most anti-SUV and anti-HUMMER zealots ascribe the appeal to some lacking, some basic need unmet in the drivers' psyche, like the following letter to the *New York Times*: "America is full of self-centered people, desperately craving attention from strangers. Hummer's general manager says, 'The people that buy this product, they're daring." What's so daring about driving a military vehicle to do errands? Riding a bicycle is daring." (Of course it would be to a Manhattanite.)

It would be impossible to reconcile the sides even before the glut of anti-SUV diatribes and acts grew into a torrent. When reduced to the facts, each side has compelling logic in its favor. America consumes 25 percent of the world's daily output of crude oil, and that oil comes with enormous geopolitical strings, linking the U.S. inseparably to rogue states and illegitimate governments. The obverse is that SUVs are a perfectly legitimate choice of vehicle for some people, and the government has no need or right to legislate which car, truck, SUV or minivan is appropriate for anyone. The last five years—the last hundred years—of progress haven't solved that paradox. And if anything, events have conspired to drive the two sides even further apart.

Firestone recalls, Ford migraines

SUV buyers in part shop for safety, translating the trucks' tall stance and aggressive grilles into a perceived safety advantage. In some measured ways the safety is real, and in others decidedly not. The latter came as a media-hyped surprise to owners of the world's most popular SUV when, in the summer of 2000, they were told their vehicles were killers.

The first cracks in the SUV's armor-plated reputation for safety appeared in late 1999, amid reports that Ford Explorer tires on vehicles sold in Venezuela were showing a tendency to crack and separate. At first, the cases were seen as isolated occurrences in a market less sophisticated than in the U.S. The miscalculation would be fatal to a hundred-year partnership between Ford and Firestone, and caused both companies a world of grief that gave SUV haters one more reason to castigate the vehicles.

The tire separations happening in Venezuela, it turned out, were happening around the world, and with increasing frequency in the United States. By the summer of 2000, Ford and Firestone huddled for more than a week before announcing that Bridgestone Firestone would recall nearly 6.5 million Firestone ATX, ATX II, and Wilderness tires constructed at one Firestone factory in Decatur, Ill. The tires had been issued as standard equipment on a range of sport-utility vehicles and pickups, mostly Ford's Explorer and Mercury Mountaineer SUVs. The National Highway Traffic Safety Administration had begun an investigation into the tires; already, some 88 deaths had been linked to the tires, which were said to lose their treads as heat built up in the tires, leading to vehicle rollovers, injuries and highway deaths.

Reports from the crisis center indicated that Firestone had been reluctant to recall the tires; the company had already suffered one such recall in the late 1970s that almost put it out of business entirely, only to be rescued by Japan's Bridgestone. Ford's Martin Inglis, vice president for North American operations at the time, said that a "war room" had been set up for ten days prior to the official recall in August 2000. Both Ford and Firestone saw the liability and public-relations nightmare ahead, and if anything, Ford had more to lose, what with its most profitable vehicle's reputation at stake.

A pair of Congressional hearings turned the Firestone recall into a true media circus on Sept. 6, 2000. "We are in the midst of a national tragedy," chimed in Rep. Billy Tauzin, R-La., who conducted the hearings at which the CEOs of both Ford and Bridgestone Firestone testified about their company's responses to the crisis.

"We know that this is a Firestone tire issue and not a vehicle issue," Ford CEO Jacques Nasser said. In contrast, Bridgestone CEO Masatoshi Ono expressed little more than his sorrow at the families' losses—though Firestone representatives would argue that Ford's Explorer design and its recommendation for lower-than-normal tire pressures were at fault for the tread separations.

The circus would end with Firestone and Ford parting ways, ending a business relationship that had stretched back into the very first years of Henry Ford's auto production. The final tally would top 271 deaths and 800 injuries. The controversy would seriously endanger the Explorer, which was critical to Ford's profitability in the 1990s: more than half of the company's profits were derived from its trucks and sport-utility vehicles, and the Explorer had been its best-selling ute since 1991.

Huffington gets personal

The groundswell of public opinion was beginning to shift against SUVs—because without the implicit safety advantage, the SUV lost a significant amount of luster. But the subtle change in the SUV's persona wouldn't sustain serious damage until a string of strident SUV critics hit the airwaves and the bookshelves, attacking sport-utes from every conceivable angle to make their own names. And first among them would be a shape-shifting gadfly who would ditch her conservative leanings for a populist platform that she would attempt to steer into the California governor's mansion, to poor effect.

Arianna Huffington's commentary on cable-news networks and in weekly columns had sported a finely honed conservative edge for years before she shifted her sights to the sport-utility vehicle and the gubernatorial race of 2003. According to the biography on her Web site, is a native of Greece, holds a masters in economics from Cambridge (U.K., not Harvard), is the author of books from *The Female Woman* in 1974 to *How to Overthrow the Government* in 2000. Prior to 2000 Huffington also appeared regularly on talk-TV programs like Bill Maher's *Politically Correct* and various news roundtables. Huffington also had been the spouse of Michael Huffington, a failed candidate in the 1994 California senatorial election in which he spent $30 million. The Huffingtons divorced in 1997, and shortly after Michael Huffington came out as a gay man—and Arianna, as a "recovering Republican."

Huffington's commentary often found her on the conservative side of political issues—she and Al Franken were the dipoles in Comedy Central's election-year coverage in 1996, in their own words the "strangest bedfellows." But as the firestorm surrounding SUV safety engulfed Ford in 2000 and echoed throughout 2001, Huffington tacked into a new populist wind and began railing against SUVs. In outlets carrying her columns and commentary, Huffington launched an anti-SUV campaign that would culminate by taking it to Detroit, literally, in 2002.

In that year, Huffington allied herself with the Detroit Project, an outfit that decried the growth of SUVs. As General Motors showed the final version of the H2 that would go on sale in the summer, Huffington and the Detroit Project unveiled a multimedia ad campaign at the Detroit auto show in January that would equate driving SUVs with supporting terrorism—a potent hypnotic in the post-9/11 era. As the Bush administration pursued war against al-Qaeda and began to publicly question old anathema Saddam Hussein's involvement in global terror, the ads publicized by Huffington put putative SUV owners into ads mouthing the unthinkable: "I helped hijack an airplane. I helped our enemies develop weapons of mass destruction."

Huffington's ads weren't the purely grass-roots efforts they were portrayed to be. The *Detroit Free Press* reported that Hollywood titans like producers Norman Lear and Steve Bing and comedian and director Larry David had bankrolled Huffington's anti-SUV campaign, paying for expensive prime-time TV commercials in major media markets.

Huffington seemed exactly the wrong person to equate fuel usage with terrorism, since her own extravagant lifestyle included homes in Washington, D.C. and California, first-class jet flights and her own SUV, though Huffington claimed to drive a Toyota Prius hybrid. But even in a hypocritical reverie, Huffington had tripped over the central issue in the rampant growth of SUVs: was too much too much? Were sport-utes good for America?

Huffington laid out the anti-SUV indictment on her own Web site, www.ariannahuffington.com, in a column entitled, "Why Oil Sheiks Love a Good HUMMER."

"Sales of the gas-guzzling, pollution-spewing, downright dangerous behemoths continue to soar," she writes. "Dealers are having a hard time keeping up with the demand for the HUMMER H2...The symbolism of these impractical machines military roots is too delicious to ignore: We go to war to protect our supply of cheap oil in vehicles that would be prohibitively expensive to operate without it."

Huffington wrote that her goal was to change the perception of driving an SUV to that of driving while drunk. "Getting loaded and getting behind the wheel went from being cool to being anti-social," she said, insinuating that merely driving an SUV was as dangerous as getting behind the wheel after a night behind the bar stool. "With luck, getting behind the wheel of a loaded gas-guzzler is about to undergo the same transformation."

But it wasn't her most extreme assertion. Later in 2002, Huffington compared the purchase of an SUV to "building a nuclear bomb for Saddam Hussein" and "buying weapons that will kill American soldiers, Marines and sailors."

High and Mighty: Unsafe at any read?

The charges against SUVs were formalized in a 2002 book aiming to be an Upton Sinclair-styled exposé of sport-utes, the *J'Accuse!* of the anti-SUV jihad. Borne by the halls of the *New York Times,* a liberal newspaper in a city more hostile to drivers than any other in America, a reporter from their Detroit outpost wrote that SUVs were more likely to endanger the lives of others than any other type of vehicle on the market.

Former *New York Times* auto reporter Keith Bradsher penned the book, *High and Mighty–SUVs: The World's Most Dangerous Vehicles and How They Got That Way,* in it blaming the SUV for a disproportionate amount of deaths because of their heft and durable construction. Bradsher accused SUVs, due to their size and strength and propensity to roll over in untrained hands, of causing as many deaths as the attacks on the World Trade Center and the Pentagon, which killed nearly 3000 people in Manhattan, D.C., and Pennsylvania almost one year to the day prior to the release of his book. "SUVs represent the biggest menace to public safety and the environment that the auto industry has produced since the bad old days of the 1960s," he intoned gravely.

Bradsher calls the SUV the "most dangerous vehicle in the world" for two main reasons. The first, that the frames of SUVs were strong enough to act as a battering ram against smaller vehicles, was true—though Bradsher conveniently omitted pickup trucks, which far outnumber SUVs, from his indictment. In addition, the frame height allows SUVs to ride over smaller cars in accidents, causing more than their fair share of injuries and deaths. Second, SUVs are also more prone to killing their occupants in rollovers, because their centers of gravity were higher than that of passenger cars.

In an e-mail interview with the author, now stationed at the *Times'* Hong Kong desk, Bradsher said that unlike cars, which meet rigorous safety standards, sport-utes aren't held to similar standards. Bradsher says he doesn't question that for some, the SUV is truly useful—just not the legions attracted to them—and even for those, the tradeoff in safety must be balanced by need.

"A small minority of SUV buyers need the vehicles in terms of towing or serious off-road driving. But SUVs provide considerable enjoyment to many. The question is whether this enjoyment should be balanced against the health risks imposed on others," he said. "Part of the problem in this whole debate is that people try to pigeonhole others as pro- or anti-SUV. A better question is whether government should be intervening in the free market by setting one set of rules for cars and a different set for light trucks."

"There are practically no safety standards at all for the two safety problems posed by SUVs: crash compatibility and rollovers," he writes.

"There is room for a crash compatibility standard that would require somewhat longer front ends for small cars as well as changes to SUVs. But as the auto industry safety engineers say, any compatibility standard would require far greater changes to SUVs than small cars. The reason is that the bulk of the crash compatibility problem comes from the fact that SUVs and pickups have front-end structures that do not match up well with the 140 million-plus cars and minivans already on the road. Making sure that their front-end structures match up better is the biggest issue for crash compatibility. Occupant protection in smaller vehicles can be addressed through all kinds of methods, including better seat belts, air bags and so forth, as well as design changes."

"I'm not a big fan of small cars—I think the world needs more large cars and minivans," he concludes. "Detroit has made tremendous progress in designing good large cars, as the book says. The golden mean would be more large but lightweight cars since size is protective in crashes while weight is deadly to other motorists. Aluminum space frames will eventually make this possible, but the manufacturing technology is not there yet at a reasonable cost, which is why few models have them now."

The difficulties of the book were nagging and substantial. For one, though SUVs are involved in more rollover accidents and deaths than cars and even minivans, overall SUVs have compiled a better safety record than many vehicle types on the road today, likely due to their robust construction. Too, there isn't any granularity to the data that tells which accidents involving SUVs were wholly the fault of the driver. And the book seems to insinuate that the mere existence of SUVs has caused more deaths than

HUMMER

Open up and say AAHhhh2.

necessary—but can anyone predict with any accuracy that substituting a passenger car for an SUV in any given accident will save any lives?

Bradsher also likely underestimates the number of people who actually need SUVs, largely because his book implies that a need must exist by narrow definitions before an SUV even becomes a rational purchase. Try explaining that to a mother of three who wants four-wheel drive and a taller vehicle because it "makes her feel safer"—or to the self-employed consultant who needs one vehicle to haul clients and weekend camping gear, too.

Whatever its historic significance, Bradsher's book marked a milestone in the anger developing toward SUVs. The sides were drawn—and now the anti-SUV crowd had a Bible from which it could quote verse and chapter. And they had only missed leading the proselytizing by a few months.

What would Jesus—or Jésus—drive?

Anti-SUV mania had become a sort of religion for a handful of highly visible celebrities and environmentalists. But to shift the argument from an ecumenical one to a truly spiritual discussion required doctrine—and a savior, apparently. Early in 2002, the Evangelical Environmental Network, "a biblically orthodox Christian environmental organization," got into the game with a Web site and a media campaign that asked the seemingly unanswerable question, "What would Jesus drive?"

Was it silly or serious? The EEN saw it merely as an extension of the religious mantra, "Lord, what would you have me do," translated on wheels as "Lord, what would you have me drive?" As stated by the group's Web manifesto, WWJD existed to help Christians and others "understand that our transportation choices are moral choices that for Christians fall under the Lordship of

Christ; and to take appropriate actions to address the problems associated with our transportation choices."

In November a group of clerics made a pilgrimage to Detroit to preach the "WWJD" gospel to automakers. The group included Rabbi David Sapirstein of the Religious Action Center of Reformed Judaism and the Rev. Dr. Bob Edgar, General Secretary of the National Council of Churches. The meeting, which was attended by execs including Ford Motor Company Chairman William Clay Ford Jr., earned much local media coverage and the obligatory pondering of the rhetorical question posed by the campaign. (The answer seemed obvious: a 15-passenger domestic van, with shoulder belts for each of the apostles except Judas.)

The seriousness and earnestness of the group's resolve demanded a tongue-in-cheek response. And with the help of a Detroit public-relations and marketing executive, the mystery was solved: Jesus—really Jésus Rivera—drove an SUV. Or so went the ad splashed across a whole page of *USA Today* in the summer of 2003. On July 14, the SUV Owners of America (SUVOA), a group formed in 1999 as a non-profit to be advocates for "24 million SUV owners in the U.S.," launched the print ad in response to the growing silliness accompanying the genuine concerns rising about SUV safety and economy.

The mind behind the satiric SUVOA campaign was Jason Vines, an Iowan drawn to Detroit as a PR exec for the former Chrysler Corporation. Vines moved up from Chrysler to Washington, where he served as an assistant to Andrew Card, President George H.W. Bush's chief of staff. He returned to automotive PR with Chrysler, then went west to take over the top communications post at Nissan's North American operations in Los Angeles, and then was elevated to vice president at Ford Motor Company—just in time to handle the Firestone tire recall. Disposed of a black sense of humor before the Firestone debacle, Vines was deposed along with former chairman Jac Nasser in November of 2001 when William Clay Ford Jr. took over the running of the family company. It was after that nightmarish turn that Vines joined Strat@comm, a PR and marketing firm that specialized in automotive clients, and joined the SUV fray.

The ad, Vines said, depicts the reality of those who choose SUVs. "Jesús Rivera drives an SUV along with 24 million other Americans who rely on their SUVs to carpool friends and family; tow boats, campers and trailers; haul home improvement supplies; and volunteer to take people to the hospital in snow emergencies." The overall campaign to smear SUVs, he said, came from small but vocal groups distorting the safety and environmental record of SUVs. "No vehicle has been demonized this much since Stephen King turned a Plymouth into Christine," said Vines during the height of the controversy.

"The truth is the largest of the SUVs have the lowest fatality rate according to the Insurance Institute for Highway Safety—end of story," said Vines, who counters suggestions that SUVs are no more useful than cars with data that points to SUVs' particular strengths: towing and carrying more passengers than normal cars— even while admitting that SUVs' higher center of gravity makes them more likely to roll in a crash. "Replacing all of the SUVs sold in the U.S. with passenger cars would save exactly one days' worth of oil," he concludes.

NHTSA checks in

When the SUV issue needed no further agitation, the government's own czar of SUV safety chimed in with public comment that would enrage SUV owners and makers and add credence to the growing cries for SUV regulation.

The Bush administration had named Dr. Jeffrey Runge as 12th head of the National Highway Traffic Safety Administration (NHTSA) in August of 2001. A physician by trade and an expert in emergency medicine concentrated in after care for car-accident victims, Runge took charge of an administration in charge of half a billion dollars and some of the vital regulations protecting consumers and drivers. However, like the first President Bush named David Souter to the Supreme Court and was surprised by his seeming conversion to the liberal wing of the court, Runge soon became an unexpected bell-ringer for safety causes.

As the new year began, the anti-SUV hysteria seemed destined to peter out. That is, until Runge made a speech that shocked Detroit and gave federal and scientific blessing to the full-court press against SUVs. At an automotive conference on January 22, 2003, Runge unveiled data and statistics that, in the agency's estimation, proved that SUVs weren't safer in accidents than many drivers assumed—in some ways, they were more dangerous.

Runge charged that of the 10,000 fatalities that came from rollover accidents each year, SUVs were becoming responsible for more than their fair share. Rollovers only accounted for three percent of accidents, he said, but 32 percent of occupant fatalities in accidents. SUVs as a group had a fatality rate from rollovers three times higher than passenger cars.

But Runge didn't stop at statistics. In an interview session after his remarks, Runge added that teens with new drivers' licenses were even more likely to roll a vehicle. "I would not put an inexperienced driver in a high, center-of-gravity vehicle (such as an SUV or pickup truck)," Runge told the audience. At another point, according to one news account, Runge suggested that he wouldn't ride in some SUVs even "if they were the last vehicle on earth."

Anti-SUV Hysteria Or, Arianna Takes On the H2

These were harsh words from the government official in charge of setting safety standards for passenger cars and light trucks. In one estimation, no agency head in Washington had ever made such a statement about the safety of sport-utility vehicles. "I was astounded he would be so honest," Rosemary Shahan, the executive director of Consumers for Auto Reliability and Safety, told the *Los Angeles Times*. "It was almost like somebody gave him truth serum."

Detroit rushed in with counterintelligence that showed some of Runge's comments had been factually correct, but one-sided. "According to real-world government crash data, compiled by the NHTSA, SUVs are two to three times more protective of their occupants in frontal, rear and side-impact crashes that make up 97.5 percent of all crashes. The major reason for fatalities in rollovers, which represent only 2.5 percent of all crashes, is due to a lack of seat belt use," GM spokesman Jay Cooney offered. Some 72 percent of those killed in fatal rollover crashes were not using safety belts, Cooney said, also adding that since SUVs grew in sales in the 1980s, sales of SUVs had risen more than 600 percent—and yet the traffic fatality rate in the U.S. had fallen by more than 50 percent.

The independent Competitive Enterprise Institute, a self-described non-partisan non-profit group, spoke out as well. The Institute argued that SUVs had a safer record that passenger cars in some cases, and were at least the equal of passenger cars. First, deaths per mile driven in the U.S. had actually decreased, the Institute said in a release. The so-called "crisis" of SUVs colliding with and riding over cars because of their height was a fallacy not supported by the numbers in light of millions of SUVs entering the U.S. fleet. And counter to the popular notion of increasing deaths in SUVs from rollover, when 3 million new SUVs were purchased in 2002, the Institute said that SUVs had one of the lowest injury rates of any type of vehicle. "NHTSA loves to focus on SUV rollovers, because this gives the agency a high-profile issue for a frequently demonized vehicle class. What NHTSA doesn't tell the public is the overall safety record of SUVs which is as good as, if not better than, that of most passenger cars," says CEI General Counsel Sam Kazman. "The agency owes the American people more candor and less gloom and doom. Given their treatment by this agency and other critics, SUV really stands for Scapegoat Utility Vehicle."

Despite the counterattack, Runge had given legitimacy to some of the arguments against SUVs–pointedly, not all of them. The anti-SUV side had a book published collating their arguments. And two weeks before Runge had dropped his bomb, Arianna Huffington and The Detroit Project launched their second ad, accusing the automakers of being able to sell 40-mpg vehicles but denying Americans the technology–a sinister and loopy assertion like the nonexistent 100-mpg carburetors Detroit supposedly kept locked away in vaults in the 1960s.

The anti-SUV hysteria had leapt into full swing once again. "We're going to try to do to the HUMMER what we did to the (Ford Excursion)," declared Daniel Becker, the Sierra Club's top energy expert, in the *Times*. "Kill it."

But from its beginning, the SUV stalkers hadn't been a byproduct of the public's hatred for SUVs–SUV sales in 2002 and 2003 continued to set records despite the Explorer/Firestone recall, the anti-SUV jihad and the rising price of gasoline. "It was never a grass-roots campaign," Vines charges. "It was a very small, very vocal group. Look at the Detroit Project – run by Fenton Communications and Arianna Huffington, people with fairly sizable bank accounts." The immediate impact on sales, Vines laughs, "was to increase them. That's because people are sick and tired of loudmouths who don't understand what we go through to put families through to school,

Anti-SUV Hysteria Or, Arianna Takes On the H2

In the 2004 model year, GM ordered up a new interior for the consumer HUMMER H1, with greatly refined materials and better sound insulation.

the fact that we work our butts off, that we want freedom – what this country is based on."

Before the end of the year, the war against SUVs would lash out in anarchy. Against the backdrop of a war against terror—a war in which the White House would move against Afghanistan first, then Iraq, seeking to obliterate the threat of another al-Qaeda attack on American soil—the war against HUMMER and SUV owners had already been joined and would soon turn violent. "The anti-SUV zealots," said a prescient Vines in 2002, "are creating an atmosphere where it's open season on SUV owners."

Chapter 9

Back to Baghdad

The phonecall Craig Mac Nab received that day in 2002 wasn't unusual. Had it been a decade before, it would have come after missions in Baghdad, or Port-Au-Prince, or Pristina. This time, the call came from parents of a soldier stationed in Kabul, Afghanistan, the opening stage of the war on terror launched in the wake of September 11. The parents, like others before them, had called AM General to thank the people who made the vehicles that saved their child's life. In that instance, Mac Nab was told that the lid on the Humvee's turret had been blown off, along with all four of the vehicle's wheels—but the soldiers emerged unharmed.

Terrorism had turned America away from navel-gazing on impeached presidents and botched election returns. After September 11, the world would be different—and the tactics of war against a shifting enemy would encompass everything from raiding accounts in American banks to returning to a fight left unsettled in 1991. At home, it also meant enduring a wholly unfamiliar level of security searches at airports, sports arenas and concert halls that drove home the point that this was a war that would be fought on American soil as well as abroad.

Seeing armed guards at Atlanta's Hartsfield International Airport may have been unnerving, or undergoing a bomb scan at Los Angeles' Staples Center unsettling—but maybe the most chilling visual of all was seeing Humvees in light camouflage, positioned around the perimeter of the Pentagon, against a backdrop of the Washington Monument and the Capitol Building and Arlington National Cemetery, on guard against more terror attacks while crews worked around the clock to repair the military's nerve center, itself a victim along with 125 Pentagon staffers and 64 on American Airlines Flight 77, which terrorists had plowed in the building's west side.

"These acts shattered steel," President Bush solemnly told the nation, "but they cannot dent the steel of American resolve."

The resolve would mean military deployment into countries suspected of harboring terrorists. And this time, the U.S military actions would unfold in prime time, live for cameras manned by "embedded" journalists reporting alongside soldiers in a fight for their lives, carted to the front in Humvees. Once again, the Humvee would be seen in the context of war, part of a twenty-four-hours-a-day campaign running on all the major broadcast and cable networks.

The Humvee marched again into war, with the U.S. military hunting down Bin Laden, Hussein, and a cartel of al-Qaeda operatives that served as the hydra heads of the terrorist network. And back on American soil, the HUMMER brand faced a war of its own from zealots convinced that the H1 and H2 were instruments of terror.

By the end of 2003, the Humvee would be a hero once more in the geopolitical arena. Arnold Schwarzenegger would be waving goodbye to his Terminator status for a while—which, if you'd seen tabloid photos of his entirely appropriately aging physique, was already sliding earthward—in exchange for loftier goals. And General Motors' team of HUMMER experts would have their hands full transforming the infant brand from a one-hit wonder into a family of vehicles with long-term appeal.

Life and death during wartime

With a meteoric rise surely must come a stumble or two, and before the day it even went on sale, the new civilian HUMMER brand debuted against a backdrop of divisive war, a gulf in patriotism over Gulf Wars one and two, and the emerging physical resistance to large SUVs from greenies as well as buyers—a "perfect storm" the whiz kids from GM's HUMMER brand could not have hoped to anticipate when they approached AM General to join the GM fold just three years before. The world had indeed changed since Sept. 11, as President George W. Bush said on countless occasions—and for HUMMER, the signs would have seemed to point to a fall.

HUMMER had marched lockstep into a maelstrom of anti-SUV hatred, economic downturn and the terrorist attacks of Sept. 11. But even on its accelerated march into production, there wasn't time to turn around. "Who knew we'd see recession, 9/11, a fall-off in sales after the first of the year in 2001, war in Iraq, gas prices spiking, and anti-SUV 'What Would Jesus Drive?' folks?" asks HUMMER's Marc Hernandez. "Analysts asked us, 'aren't you missing the beam launching during the recession?' Hell, if we knew and could not launch during a recession, don't you think we would?"

All of these factors were big worries until early sales numbers began to roll in. The most sensitive component of all those worries

HUMMER

wasn't the war on terror, though. HUMMER officials had been wise to position their vehicle not solely on its military heritage; it had been calculated to draw on the essence of the H1 and the HUMMER icon—but without the uncomfortable association with war. Clinicked and tested and virtually pre-approved by its intended audience, the H2 was surgically crafted to appeal with only the passing reference to war and peace in its seven-slot grille.

"Of course, we realize the connection to the military images. That's why we bought the brand," says HUMMER spokesman Pete Ternes. But the HUMMER team knew it couldn't just be overtly patriotic. "It can trip you up," says Mike DiGiovanni.

"It can be both a negative and a positive," agrees Hernandez. "The military is a part of our heritage. We will not run or hide from it. The vehicle has the DNA that it does, and it's something we're very proud of." At the same time, Hernandez says, HUMMER has been particularly careful in the post-9/11 era not to tread on its military heritage. "We don't drape the American flag over it, or market it as, 'this is the vehicle who kicked so and so's behind,' whether it's Saddam [Hussein] or someone else."

But HUMMER executives had to pay special attention for sensitivities that no other brand had to, since its cousin the Jeep. "There was some question, some sense that we were maybe exploiting the war in Iraq. People would turn on CNN and see a HUMMER ad, then cut to Iraq and you'd see Humvees moving down the road. The reality is that we weren't going to stop advertising," Hernandez says, during the critical launch of the new H2. "Given our demographics, we haven't changed our mix of advertising—it's just that people are watching a lot more news, surfing the war itself, tuning in. That's where we were, before the war and during the war."

Some journalists openly questioned whether GM had boosted its own image on the back of the war effort. Hernandez and

DiGiovanni both recall conversations with media and other Detroit executives echoing what they say was a common misperception: "'I hear your sales are through the roof,' they asked." The truth, they indicate, is that the sales barely changed during the entire year and a half it had been on sale through the end of 2003, averaging roughly 2900 units per month for each month in the year. In fact, near the end of 2003, GM was compelled to offer rebates to clear out older H2 utes to make room for the coming 2004 model.

Lightning battles and global wars

Reducing two global conflicts into a few pages of text does disrespect to the nearly thousand soldiers who have lost their lives in the conflicts. In both cases, the immediate consequences of the wars were clear, but the aftereffects in constant evolution.

The wars in Afghanistan and in Iraq in 2002 and early 2003 were the opening salvos in a "war on terror" that, it was and still is fervently hoped, will cleave Hamas from its underground river of funding, separate al-Qaeda from the technology and weapons it seeks to catapult Islam to the world's dominant religion, and if successful, would put the Bush Doctrine of pre-emptive strikes against terror in the history books alongside the Monroe Doctrine that first outlined the U.S.'s grand ambition for hemispherical dominance in the early 1800s.

President Bush's policy on terrorism expanded the scope of pursuit to include not only the individuals responsible for heinous acts like the World Trade Center bombings in 1993 and their destruction in 2001, but also the countries that harbored them. With that policy of pre-emption, Bush's political foes galvanized against the war effort and against Bush's willingness to go it alone in the war on terror, with or without the express consent of the United Nations. The divisions in the country already seen from the election in

2000–where the U.S. Supreme Court had stepped in to clarify Florida election law to the dismay of the Gore campaign–became much sharper. The elite class was split again. In Lutzian terms the thinking elite saw the coming wars as illegal actions not endorsed by the international community (which in reality amounted to France, Germany and Russia) and the "doing" elite, which saw the pursuit of terrorism around the globe as a new world war in its dawning stages, one which the U.S. had to win to survive.

The engagement in Afghanistan came quickly after September 11, in October of 2001, when American and British intelligence had confirmed that al-Qaeda's chief instigator, Osama Bin Laden, had coordinated the attacks on America from the remote caves of Afghanistan's southeast provinces along the border with Pakistan. Bin Laden had the blessing of the fundamentalist Taliban regime, which ruled Afghanistan through an extreme interpretation of Islam of forced conversion of non-Muslims or their extermination, seizing power over the eternally impoverished, landlocked country in the decade after the Soviet Union withdrew from their invasion in 1989. Bin Laden also had been implicated in the 1998 bombing of U.S. embassies in the capitals of Kenya and Tanzania and the bombing of the U.S.S. *Cole* off the coast of Yemen. President Bush had demanded the Taliban give the U.S. access to inspect terrorist training camps in the landlocked country, and demanded the Taliban turn over suspected al-Qaeda operatives in the country.

Led by General Tommy Franks, a coalition of United Nations-endorsed nations joined the U.S. in Operation Enduring Freedom. On Oct. 7, U.S. and British forces began bombing Taliban targets in Afghanistan. By Nov. 13, the Taliban had evacuated Kabul and though engagements would continue periodically–some critics say because the war plan in the country was underfunded and

Back to Baghdad

The Air Force is just one branch of the U.S. armed forces that depends on the Humvee.

undermanned—the Taliban would be out of effective control of the nation, while a Western-backed governing council led by Hamid Karzai worked to draft a new constitution for the once tribally governed country. However, the chief target of the campaign, Osama Bin Laden, remained at large, on some occasions thought to have been killed in raids or bombings, on other occasions delivering videotaped and audible messages of no clear time. The shadowy opponent feared in the anti-terror campaign seemed to still be alive.

In 2002, as the Afghanistan operations changed gears from invasion to nation-building, the Bush administration began to send signals that Iraq would be the next nation to suffer for its covert backing of terrorism. Sequels usually aren't as good as the original stories, but in this case the conclusion would be altogether more satisfying for this President Bush.

The suspicions of Hussein's links to international terror had dated back to Operation Desert Storm, as had Hussein's recalcitrance at declaring his weaponry and allowing unfettered access to sensitive sites within Iraq to United Nations inspectors. Hussein had ignored 12 U.N. directives since the end of the first Gulf War to disarm and prove that its weapons of mass destruction had been disposed of in a regular way. Among them, Iraq was known to have nerve agents and biological weapons—and the threat of nuclear technology was thought to be sought out by Hussein. The Iraqi regime also had brutalized its own people, and intelligence operations around the world had linked the Iraqis to global terror campaigns like those from al-Qaeda.

In the fall of 2002, the Bush administration started the first phase of the campaign against Iraq by gaining approval from Congress for military action against Iraq with the encouragement to involve the United Nations. Then on November 8, 2002, the United

Nations Security Council approved unanimously the Security Council Resolution 1441, which gave Iraq "a final opportunity to comply with its disarmament obligations" and threatened "serious consequences" if they did not. After an intense period of returning U.N. inspectors, a blizzard of paperwork and denials from the Hussein regime on the extent of its weapons programs, the Bush administration decided that Hussein's cat-and-mouse game would end. In March of 2003, the United Nations refused to authorize another resolution explicitly giving the U.S. and Great Britain the right to use force—a rebuff that the nations sidestepped in creating a "coalition of the willing" that entered Iraq by force on March 20, 2003.

The Humvee was central in military operations once more. As in previous campaigns, it served as a sort of "mobile foxhole," according to *USA Today's* David Kiley, as well as ambulance, police vehicle, armament carrier, missile launcher, telecom trailer and recon machine. But now, the Humvee would also be bait. This time the Department of Defense permitted reporters to be "embedded" along with the military campaign; the Associated Press followed in a typical campaign meant to flush out Iraqi resistance with U.S. Marine Lieut. Colonel Bryan P. McCoy, 40, midway through the three-week march to Baghdad. Humvees were used in this battle, for instance, to draw out Iraqi fighters south of Baghdad and leave the capital largely unprotected by serious armored force:

> *"We're going chumming," he told the wire service. "We're going to throw some bait into the water and see if the sharks will come out." The sharks are an estimated 3,000 Iraqi soldiers in Diwaniyah, a city of 300,000 people 75 miles southeast of Baghdad, where the 1991 southern Shi'ite rebellion against Saddam Hussein first started.*

But as the war had fractured global diplomacy and the civilian sentiment back in the U.S. And the second Iraqi War, "Operation Iraqi Freedom," would be covered by the media across the spectrum, from raging against the war machine to flag-waving for the Bush Doctrine and the U.S.' international might. But the attacks of Sept. 11 had punctured the invincibility of America that had gradually been rebuilt since the Vietnam era—and the Humvee, like the rest of the military, was seen as vulnerable even though the goal of the mission in Iraq, to remove Hussein from power, took only about three weeks.

The war had its casualties and soldiers in Humvees were among them—especially in the months after the initial campaign, when Hussein had disappeared into the countryside and insurgents, thought to be terrorists recruited to push the western forces out of the country, were conducting terror raids against the military. The *New York Times* chronicled one such attack in midsummer in which one American soldier was killed and three were wounded when their Humvee was bombed as they drove under a bridge in central Baghdad. The bomb exploded, leaving a crater in the sidewalk and spraying the vehicle with shrapnel. The two soldiers riding on the left side of the vehicle took the brunt of the blast; the two on the right side walked away. The timing and placement of the bomb suggested a device larger than the grenade, the paper suggested—and the timing suggested an ambush of the kind the coalition forces would face increasingly often in the months to come even though President Bush, aboard the aircraft carrier *U.S.S. Abraham Lincoln* had declared an end to combat operations on May 1, 2003.

For the majority of soldiers at the wheel of every flavor of Humvee, the outcomes were more favorable. AM General spokesman Craig Mac Nab received many more calls from parents of soldiers, as he usually did during combat operations, thanking the company for the armored Humvees that had saved their child's life. The only controversy the Humvees endured during Iraqi Freedom were that there weren't enough of them—specifically, the up-armored versions. Some estimates of the Humvee fleet of about 140,000 vehicles placed about 10,000 in service in Iraq and only 2000 of those were up-armored, meaning they added armored crew compartments, two-inch thick bulletproof windows, a roof gun turret, gun shields, and upgraded suspensions.

The objective in Iraq had been completed, but by May it was clear a guerilla war had sprung up in the void left behind by the Hussein regime. Inspectors scanned the country for suspected weapons of mass destructions, but none were uncovered. Hussein had been evicted from his lavish palaces and forced into hiding, but still hadn't been captured.

Homeland security

While up-armored Humvees became a battlefield necessity in Iraq, and for one of the Humvee's suppliers, it became a boon. O'Gara-Hess & Eisenhardt had been retrofitting Humvees with additional protection ever since the tragic losses endured in Somalia in Operation Restore Hope. With the action in Iraq, the company boosted its build rate for the M1114 by 25 percent—the busiest it had been since the Bosnian crisis in 1996.

Customer-driven and likely war-driven, O'Gara began offering a reinforced HUMMER H2 in 2003, adding it quickly to its fleet. "Just one look at an H2 and you know it is a substantial vehicle, one providing an excellent platform for armoring and protecting its occupants," Gary Allen, general manager of O'Gara's mobile security division, told the AP. The company that first built bulletproofing into the limousine for President Harry S. Truman, now could build in protection for 50 Cent and other rappers, celebrities and select paranoiacs.

On the H2, the protection system uses "opaque" armor—bulletproof glass, for the civilians on the other side of the ordering desk—and reinforced steel and composite panels and body pieces. All the doors, roof rails, pillars floor and roof are beefed up and multi-layered ballistic glass is added to make the H2 protect its occupants from gunnery up to an AK-47. At the same time the buyer—whether a Colombian importer/exporter or a head of state—can order interior upgrades like DVD entertainment and audio systems as well as wood trim.

Meanwhile, the military Humvee had been given a larger role in homeland defense. Outfitted with the Avenger air defense system, for example, Humvees were stationed around the perimeter of Washington to guard the White House, the Pentagon and other government buildings with radar and the ability to rapidly fire eight Stinger missiles.

Washington would not be the only territory deemed critical to defend. Within the Bush Administration's definition of the war on terror, the U.S. itself was a battlefield where incursions could come at any moment from anonymity. Intelligence and counterintelligence were the chief weapons of the war at home, but the Humvee played a role equally as important to the searches conducted at major sports games or the sometimes onerous security measures that ground down the nation's air travel to a nerve-jarring halt.

The 2002 Salt Lake City Winter Olympics were typical of the Humvee's newfound duties as protector of the homeland. The Naval Research Laboratory in Washington, D.C., outfitted one of its Humvees as a mobile communications lab and stationed it at the Olympics to instantly relay information back to Washington to prevent a terrorist strike. Similar vehicles had been prepared in the days following Sept. 11, but stood down as the threat of more immediate attacks subsided. The NRL set up the Humvee with capabilities including two-way satellite links, mobile radio networking and its own cellular telephone network, giving the specialized Humvee the capability to transmit telephone signals and data anywhere—useful in protecting the 70,000 daily visitors to the Games in case the city's links to the outside world were ruptured in an attack.

War comes home

In the summer of 2003, as violence escalated in Iraq, the anti-SUV jihad opened a new chapter in the war against sport-utes. Signaled by the words of the Sierra Club and Arianna Huffington, the cultural campaign against SUVs turned violent.

At the end of July, the Sierra Club took its anti-SUV campaign into squarely anti-HUMMER territory. The environmental organization started a Web site, www.hummerdinger.com, that was a parody of news sites. In a kludgy attempt to mimic the style of sites like TheOnion.com, a satiric news Web site, the Sierra Club penned articles for the site with headlines like, "GM celebrates HUMMER's state-of-the-art 1950s engine technology with some of today's hottest stars," using Fabian and Pat Boone as the H2's hip counterparts. The site also featured a 30-second TV spot that mocked HUMMER's ad campaign, "Like Nothing Else," with the tagline, "Pollutes Like Nothing Else." The campaign didn't have the soundbite quality of the Sierra Club's smear campaign against the Ford "Valdez" Excursion. GM countered that the HUMMER H2, at 40,000 trucks a year, wouldn't have that big an effect on the world. "Any effect that HUMMER could have is minuscule," GM spokesman Pete Ternes said. "It's clear they are just using its popularity to promote their cause and not really to make a difference."

HUMMER

In action in Afghanistan.

Within a month, the sentiments of the Sierra Club and Arianna Huffington would be followed by anarchic violence that left one businessman losing $1 million in assets. On the night of August 22, 2003, an unknown number of vandals associated with the Earth Liberation Front took to Clippinger Chevrolet/HUMMER dealership in West Covina, a satellite city of Los Angeles, and torched a warehouse filling with 20 HUMMER H2s, burning $1 million worth of inventory. Other SUVs on the lot were damaged, spray-painted with slogans like "Fat, Lazy Americans" and "ELF." The dealerships, owned by Ziad Alhassen, weren't the only ones struck – a Ford dealership in the area had the FBI involved looking for two men caught by a surveillance camera spray-painting vehicles.

The ELF, which calls itself an "an international underground organization that uses direct action in the form of economic sabotage to stop the destruction of the natural environment," claimed that in that single night in August, it damaged about 40 vehicles across the Southland. The HUMMERs weren't singled out – but the most violent damage came to them, which Mercedes-Benz M-Class SUVs were tagged with "terrorist," "killer" slogans, and some in Duarte, Calif, tagged with "gross polluter" and "we (heart) pollution." With no small amount of self-righteousness, the ELF proudly claims on its Web site that since 1997, the network has caused $100 million in damages "to entities who profit from the destruction of life and the planet."

Across the Los Angeles metro area, SUV dealers were forced to fortify their businesses with security guards, new protective measures, and round-the-clock attention. And on the Earth Liberation Front Web site, the home page showed the fruits of their labor – the charred carcass of an H2. According to the Los Angeles *Times*, the organization also claimed responsibility for SUV attacks that took place in Pennsylvania earlier in the year.

On Sept. 12, the Federal Bureau of Investigation thought they had their man. Joshua Thomas Connole, a 25-year-old environmental activist acknowledged on the ELF Web Site, was arrested at his home in Pomona, in connection with the firebombing of the HUMMER dealership. Connole, a warehouse worker at a company making solar-energy panels, was arrested outside a home that he and five others had turned into a collective named Regen.v5, a group dedicated to anti-war, anti-U.S. activism and environmentalism, according to the Los Angeles *Times*. But before Connole could post $825,000 bail he was released. The West Covina police department told the *Times* it couldn't present all the evidence they had to prosecutors within the required 48-hour window; the evidence reportedly included videotape of Connole on the premises of the dealership. Connole was freed on Sept. 15, but remained a suspect in the case through 2003.

A poorly timed policy

HUMMERs slipped further from their war-hero standing in the middle of 2003, as President Bush used tax relief to jolt the economy out of the doldrums. One particular tax cut, intended to help farmers and other drivers of heavy-duty vehicles write off their equipment faster had the unintended effect of making large SUVs the best tax writeoff in history.

In the tax code prior to the Bush administration's tinkering, small business owners had been allowed to depreciate the cost of new heavy equipment including vehicles or deduct the entire amount in a single year, so long as it came in at less than $25,000. As a part of the hotly contested Jobs and Growth Act of 2003, the single-year deduction for equipment went up to $100,000—meaning that a doctor, lawyer or consultant could purchase a HUMMER H1 and deduct nearly its entire $110,000 pricetag in the first year. The most visible large SUV on the market stuck to the image of the deduction as a sop to the wealthy, even though the "HUMMER of a tax break" applied equally to BMW's X5, Land Rover's Range Rover, and virtually every large American-made SUV and pickup truck.

"Oh, you've got to be kidding," Atlanta-area HUMMER dealer Skip Barnett told the *Detroit News*. "That would make a HUMMER practically free."

The deduction, still on the books at the end of 2003 despite attempts to remove it from the tax code by Democrats and Republicans alike, expires in 2006. Passenger cars aren't included.

California, recalled

A war of a different kind was playing itself out at home, not in terms of homeland security but in terms of election drama. The Presidential race of 2000 had given the country a taste of brinkmanship at the ballot box—and thanks to a populist measure in the California constitution written back in 1911, California would be plunged into a recall melodrama that fittingly ended in an actor retaking the governor's mansion—to add to his collection of homes around the world, airplanes, custom-made suits and watches and his personal fleet of HUMMERs, including the very first one sold to a civilian.

"I'll be back," Arnold Schwarzenegger had intoned in his role as the T2000, in *Terminator 2*. And indeed, Arnold had been back in his role as the Terminator in the second sequel, *Terminator 3: Rise of the Machines*, that opened in theaters around the country on July 2, 2003.

But like the slippery, shape-shifting character in the film, Arnold was morphing himself, away from the action-star hero and HUMMER buff into a politician poised to jump in the race if California voters decided by petition to recall their governor.

California, the world's sixth-largest economy, had plunged into a $36 billion deficit, thanks to economic mismanagement, an energy crisis in 2000-2001 that led to rolling blackouts across the Golden State, and several state initiatives that hampered the state's ability to pay its way out of crises. Or, so went the arguments for recalling Gov. Gray Davis, a policy wonk with an unfortunately timed lack of charisma. Conservatives had seized on the idea of a recall election—provided for in a 1911 revision of the California constitution—that could oust the Governor from office and give state Republicans a decent shot at reclaiming the office they held during much of the 1960s and 1970s with Ronald Reagan, the 1980s through George Deukmejian and the 1990s behind Pete Wilson. Davis, a Democrat, had taken office in 1998 in a landslide, when California was riding high on the dot-com boom in the Bay Area—but in the dot-com bust of the early 2000s, his job was on the line.

By July 23, 2003, a motion to put a recall vote before the state's voters gained the number of signatures needed. Needing more than 850,000 votes to get a recall, advocates collected more than 1.3 million valid autographs. By the quirks written into the recall law, some 135 candidates qualified for the recall ballot, everyone from Lieutenant Gov. Cruz Bustamante to child actor Gary Coleman to porn queen Mary Carey—to actor and rising Republican star Arnold Schwarzenegger, ambassador for the HUMMER brand. Strange as it might seem to an election, the HUMMER connection became a revolving-door joke and a motif throughout the election—particularly when the undercurrent of war in Iraq was real and Arnold was under fire for not one, but a passel of allegedly inappropriate HUMMERs.

Schwarzenegger's run seemed improbable to many, and in any other state in the union unconditioned to celebrities, it might have sunk under its own preposterousness. But Schwarzenegger has a keen sense of timing: the very momentum of the recall campaign worked in his favor, since his name among all the candidates had the best name recognition. And the total-recall campaigner was no longer the *Total Recall* action hero that plugged Sharon Stone twice in one scene. Schwarzenegger was an astute businessman who had built a financial empire out of a bodybuilding career, had the voice of the American immigrant myth down to the thick Austrian accent, still had his movie-star looks in his 50s, and had the right political connections by marrying into the Kennedy family in the 1980s to learn about how to manipulate and work the gears of the political machinery necessary to win.

His campaign wouldn't be without its thudding moments: announcing his candidacy on Jay Leno's *Tonight Show* came across as too pat and too Hollywood, but Schwarzenegger made no more visible mistakes in what would turn to be a less personal, more issue-driven campaign than many expected.

Arnold's HUMMER problems were twofold, but neither would keep him from serious contention in the gubernatorial race. Allegations that he had fondled and misappropriated body parts of unwilling women during his marriage were rampant. But in California and as a star, the stories didn't linger.

But the HUMMER issue was a larger, thornier problem in the state that virtually led the way in lowering emissions and raising fuel economy by dint of legislation. Arnold was indelibly linked to the HUMMER brand and at least one other candidate planned to use it against him. As he began his campaign after announcing his candidacy on August 6, after a summer in which his *Terminator 3: Rise of the Machines* had done decent box-office business, he began in earnest to patrol the state for votes. Protestors did Arnold a big favor by following him early on; the constant crowds chanting "A HUMMER isn't Green!" coupled with the celebrity gawkers gave Schwarzenegger even more media pull, sucking the air out of candidacies by arguably more qualified candidates like Republican State Senator Tom McClintock.

Schwarzenegger faced real campaign issues and his spokesperson role for HUMMER ran his campaign right into the green issues that gripped California. But as the rest of his campaign would show—as in the allegations of sexual misconduct—Schwarzenegger was able to skirt around the issue with a call to action, because the campaign was so brief.

When it came to his women problems, Schwarzenegger said he would hire a private investigator to investigate claims that he fondled women. When it came to the HUMMER, though, Schwarzenegger co-opted the greens by promising to convert one of his Hummers to hydrogen power and to build a network of fueling stations for hydrogen vehicles along the state's highways by 2010. Schwarzenegger also announced that, as governor, he would install hydrogen fueling stations every 20 miles on California interstates, giving the nascent clean-air technology an infrastructure critical to their acceptance. His goal for building the network by 2010 was considered just as aggressive as any number of characters he played in film, since even leaders in hydrogen fuel-cell technology didn't see them entering mass production before 2010.

Hydrogen vehicles—touted by some as the future of transportation—use hydrogen gas to produce electricity by passing the gas through a membrane and capturing the energy released in a chemical reaction as electricity. Automakers from Toyota to General Motors to BMW are hoping to harness hydrogen power, but so-called "fuel-cell" vehicles aren't expected to be in mass production before the end of the decade. Nevertheless, Schwarzenegger's promise held water with many—save for the local Sierra Club, which claimed that Schwarzenegger's promotion of the HUMMER brand meant his proposals couldn't be trusted. But Republican governors preceding Schwarzenegger had not been laggards on green issues, either: both Pete Wilson and George Deukmejian had spearheaded legislation to tighten the laws governing vehicle emissions in the state.

Schwarzenegger's green gambit didn't lessen the pressure on him, particularly from Arianna Huffington, whose campaign seemed more targeted against Schwarzenegger than it did for the office of governor. Huffington's participation with the Detroit Project to condemn SUVs as tools that funded terrorism had not abated by the time she joined the race in August. As her own Web site, www.ariannahuffington.com, argued, the governor's race was "the hybrid versus the HUMMER." Huffington, who owned a hybrid Toyota Prius rate at 51 mpg, even animated her campaign theme in a short film played on her Web site. The amateurish, laughable vignette showed Schwarzenegger piloting his Hummer without regard for the environment: "Nobody can catch me, you deadbeat Huffington!" he yells as Huffington tries to keep up in her Prius. His "gas-belching" HUMMER has to stop for gas often, which has Arnold fuming by the end of the short: "You stupid HUMMER!" Bizarre, unintentionally hilarious and somewhat loony, the film alternately suggests an oil-industry conspiracy, Schwarzenegger's lack of regard for the environment and Huffington's semi-serious aims at the highest office in California.

But Huffington would hold her best-crafted one-liners for a historic debate held September 24 in Sacramento—the state's first debate that featured candidates from other political parties, like the Green Party's Peter Camejo, Huffington, Lt. Gov. Cruz Bustamante, and Schwarzenegger and Tom McClintock. Bustamante and Schwarzenegger, running in the lead in polls to the day of the debate. Huffington closed in on Arnold in the debate, criticizing he and McClintock and state Republicans for allowing corporate tax loopholes to continue. Schwarzenegger responded that he could "drive my HUMMER" through the loopholes Huffington had used to reduce her taxes over the prior two years.

"I was writing and researching a book, and I wasn't making $20 million violent movies," she countered.

Huffington alluded to Schwarzenegger's female problems when he interrupted her during an exchange: "This is the way you treat women. We know that. But not now." The moderator ruled her remarks a personal attack and allowed Schwarzenegger a one-line rebuttal of his own: "I would just like to say that I just realized that I have a perfect part for you in *Terminator 4*."

"Ladies and gentlemen, this is not Comedy Central," moderator Stan Statham said. But that wasn't entirely apparent to the rest of the world watching a populist revolt in action. Californians were angry, and polls indicated as many as 67 percent of those surveyed would look to the debates to make their choice in the coming recall election. Schwarzenegger hadn't struck any ferocious blows, but neither did he suffer the slings of the other four candidates. If nothing, the process had clearly sidelined all candidates except for him and the Lieutenant Governor.

It was no surprise than on September 30, just a week later, Arianna Huffington withdrew from the race. Appearing on *Larry King Live*, Huffington revealed her real agenda in running. "I'm pulling out and I am going to concentrate every ounce of time and energy over the next week working to defeat the recall, because I've realized that that's the only way now to defeat Arnold Schwarzenegger," she told King. "I was against the recall on principle. I've always believed that this is not the way to run a democracy. But I saw the opportunity provided to elect with a simple plurality an independent, progressive governor. Now that

Break out the snorkel: HUMMER H1s can wade in water deep enough to swim in.

HUMMER

this is clear this is not going to happen, I believe that there's a clear and present danger, Larry, when it comes to the Pete Wilson Republican forces using Schwarzenegger, really, to get back in control of the state, because Arnold Schwarzenegger is a charming man. He's a nice man, but really, he has no idea how to run a state, and he is going to be run by the very forces that basically have destroyed so much of California."

And less than a week before the election was held, the SUV owners had spoken out politically in a poll from the Web site Kelley Blue Book, www.kbb.com, a provider of car pricing information. The Kelley survey found that support for the recall of Gray Davis was highest among SUV and pickup owners, 71 percent of which were in favor of removing the governor, with sedan owners at 65 percent and minivan and wagon drivers nearly split at 56 percent in favor of a recall. When the polls results were split by candidate, Schwarzenegger got the most votes from those polled at 41 percent—but also he received most of his backing from SUV drivers in the poll. Sedan drivers tended to favor Bustamante. The poll results broke out as follows, with percentages of votes followed by the candidates and the vehicles driven by people who voted for them in the unscientific poll:

    41.4%   Arnold Schwarzenegger:
                non-luxury imports, SUVs
    27.1%   Tom McClintock: luxury vehicles, pickups
    25.5%   Cruz Bustamante: non-luxury imports, sedans
    2.0%   Peter Camejo: non-luxury imports,
                minivan/station wagons
    1.6%   Arianna Huffington: luxury vehicles, sedans
    1.4%   Larry Flynt, erotic publisher:
                non-luxury domestics, pickups

0.4%   Mary "Mary Carey" Cook, porn star:
         luxury vehicles, sedans
0.4%   Gary Coleman, child actor:
         non-luxury domestics, pickups

The results would come eerily close to the final results of the recall election, just days away.

A world in confusion faced voters and drivers by the fall of 2003. With about a year left before he would face re-election, President Bush had engaged the world in a game of confrontation aimed at reducing towers of failed diplomacy to rubble and truly engaging the "new world order" his father had championed for the Middle East and had been unable to deliver. Soldiers had died in Afghanistan and in Iraq, although in both cases the U.S. could rightfully claim, with or without the support of the United Nations, that the paradigm had shifted, and that global terrorism would not be allowed free rein.

Humvees were back in action—in the sands of Iraq and the wintry Khyber Pass in Afghanistan—and yet in their home country they were targeted as un-patriotic. One of their fathers had moved from the starry realm into perhaps one more grounded in reality—though anyone paying attention to the nutty electoral maneuverings in California could rightly have chalked up the recall election, scheduled for October 7, 2003, to one more instance of the Golden State being the crazy aunt in the attic no one talked about, instead of the elitist-backed populist outrage it really represented.

In both cases, epochal changes were happening—and the Humvee played a role in it all. And all the while, the H2 enjoyed the kind of sales success envied by other niche products like the flopping Ford Thunderbird and the sagging VW Beetle. HUMMER was evolving rapidly into a mature brand, even while the potent symbols of its birth—Arnold and Saddam—were, literally, on the run.

Chapter 10

As Good As It Gets

On October 7, California's voters did what would have been unthinkable just two years prior to the state's first successful recall election: they elevated Arnold Schwarzenegger to the office of governor of the most populous state in the country and put the Terminator in charge of one of the top ten economies on the planet. Gov. Gray Davis was ousted on the ballot's first question by a 55-percent majority. Needing only to garner the most votes, Schwarzenegger easily outpolled his nearest opponent, Cruz Bustamante, with 3.74 million votes to the lieutenant governor's 2.43 million votes.

Schwarzenegger's election was certified in mid-November, and in a quiet ceremony he was inaugurated in the state capital of Sacramento, delivering an address devoid of the one-liners and movie quotes with which his campaign had been riddled. The new Governor was serious and studied in declaring that his administration was intent on not letting politics rule the day:

> "We have tough choices ahead. The first choice that we must make is the one that will determine our success. Shall we rebuild our state together or shall we fight amongst ourselves, create even deeper divisions and fail the people of California? Well let me tell you something, the answer is clear. For the people to win, politics as usual must lose."

No mention of HUMMER was made, of course—since Schwarzenegger had declared his candidacy in August, Schwarzenegger stopped doing events and public appearances on behalf of General Motors. The status of his deal with GM and his Inner City Games foundation remains intact. But he is not expected to appear on GM or HUMMER's behalf during his term, nor will he be starring in any films during his tenure as governor.

The people at GM's HUMMER brand weren't surprised by Schwarzenegger's run for governor. "He's a natural-born leader, he wants to change humanity for the better," says HUMMER's DiGiovanni. "What he's saying about what he wants to do with California…he believes it in his heart and soul. It's not fabricated."

Whether Schwarzenegger would be able to turn around California's finances—or even gain some measure of control over the state's Democratically top-heavy legislature remained uncertain in the months after he took office. But he had managed the kind of career jump attempted by many and successfully managed by few—like Schwarzenegger's Republican forefather, Ronald Reagan.

Those same Democrats probably thought they been drafted into their own war on terror within the Golden State. Meanwhile, across the globe, Osama Bin Laden's whereabouts remained a mystery to U.S. intelligence. And though the real war on terror had achieved some big objectives in less than a year, two of the biggest prizes continued to elude U.S. forces while the world waited to see if the Bush administration's policy of intervention would cure the Middle East of its explosive tendencies.

"We got him"
Then on December 13, at about 8 p.m., U.S. forces operating on tips divulged by some of Saddam Hussein's closest associates were directed to an area near Adwar, outside his birthplace of Tikrit, site of one of his most extravagant palaces. About 600 4th Infantry Division soldiers and special operations forces circled an area on a rural farm, where they saw two men fleeing and found $750,000 in U.S. $10 bills on the site. Forces cordoned off the area, focusing on an area northwest of a walled compound containing a lean-to and a hut.

Reports said that a simple fiber tipped off the troops. Brushing away the dirt near the suspicious fiber, troops found a Styrofoam panel and lifted it to uncover a 6x8 "spider hole." In a few shocking seconds, the man trapped beneath the surface raised his hands in surrender, with panicky troops unsure what or who would rise from the pit.

"I am Saddam Hussein, president of Iraq," the man told his captors in broken English. "I am willing to negotiate."

"President Bush sends his regards," a special forces soldier replied.

Hussein, so germ-phobic his visitors would be required to bathe before being received, had been hiding in the spider hole. A plastic pipe vented fresh air in, and a small fan circulated air in his underground prison.

Bearded, dazed and defiant, according to witnesses, Hussein was held in the area for about an hour before being airlifted to a nearby location by helicopter. Word trickled out to the news media late on Saturday evening, U.S. time—and on Sunday afternoon in Baghdad, Lt. Gen. Ricardo Sanchez and Paul Bremer, the chief U.S. administrator in Iraq, held a news conference announcing his capture.

"Ladies and gentlemen...we got him," Bremer announced, as a videotape of Saddam being checked by a physician played on a screen. The joy of Iraqi journalists spoke louder than Bremer or any American sentiment; some of the Iraqi journalists leapt to their feet, shouting in defiance, "Death to Saddam!"

HUMMER bears fruit

In a short twenty-five years in existence, the Humvee has spawned the civilian Hummer, an entirely new HUMMER brand, and a worldwide image instantly identifiable on television, in print and on the brim of a backward baseball cap.

For the U.S. military, the Humvee has become as ubiquitous as the World War II-era jeeps. Used by all the branches of the military, the war wagon has been configured in every imaginable way to fight, flee or inflict serious damage on opposing forces. Humvees have served as missile launchers and machine guns, grenade launchers and mobile intelligence labs. Per the Army's specifications for its Objective Force, the Humvee is responsive, deployable, agile, versatile, lethal, survivable, and sustainable. Other Humvees are put into the field for non-military but equally important uses—by border patrols, park services, and as fire and rescue vehicles.

In its third generation, the Humvee keeps improving, too. AM General engineers proudly point out that everything is different in today's Humvee from the original A0 model. Now on version A2, AM General has made running improvements that have changed virtually every part on the vehicle. Only the basic design parameters remain the same. Sun visors, for example, were added after Operation Desert Storm. The latest Humvees meet 2004 emissions regulations, gets a new cooling stack and anti-lock brakes—and version A3 is on the way.

At the same time, the military still uses vehicles other than the Humvee where appropriate. A Humvee just isn't right for every mission. Picking up the mail, for instance, is grunt work left to military-grade Chevy Blazers, some 70,000 of them requisitioned by the government.

While it continues to evolve, the Humvee is destined to be a part of the American military for years to come. The current AM General production contract runs through 2007. With A3 models on the way, AM General expects there may be an A4 model, as the Pentagon has dropped research for now on a potential Humvee replacement. The Pentagon expects to deploy the vehicles through 2013; "you can see them buying them Humvees into the 2020s," says AM General's Mac Nab.

The Humvee may also turn out to be something of a savior for Renco Group owner Ira Rennert. Its contracts in hand, and money flowing in from the licensing of the brand to General Motors, it has become an asset rather than a massive liability on his ledgers. Renco bought AM General in 1992 for about $133 million; in August 2004, they reached a deal worth an estimated $930 million to sell effective control of AM General to billionaire Ronald Perelman's MacAndrews & Forbes Holdings Inc. Perelman's group will have effective control over the Humvee maker once the deal is completed. The agreement to build GM's HUMMER H2 under contract will remain in place, as will AM General's management team, according to AM General.

It also has benefited the career of GM's DiGiovanni. Despite an early-2004 slump in H2 sales, DiGiovanni will become executive director of strategic marketing, a new position in the company. Susan Docherty, a former brand marketing director for the Cadillac Escalade, will take over his slot in the HUMMER-sphere.

For General Motors, HUMMER has polished its credentials as a responsive, market-savvy company with the engineering brilliance, customer intuition and engineering capability to execute world-class vehicles—a reputation it thought it had built to last in the 1960s. The intervening decades gradually chipped away at GM's dominance and by the time the HUMMER notion drifted through the halls of GM's styling department, the cupboards were bare.

HUMMER brought with it a brand name virtually unsullied by bad old products, a common complaint for GM, as well as a reputation for toughness forged around the world thanks to the U.S. military. "Land Rover has its heritage from the Boer Wars, Jeep draws its heritage primarily from World War II and has had no military presence since then. In terms of ruggedness and credentials, HUMMER is now the top brand in the world, easily," said GM vice chairman, Bob Lutz.

GM proved with the HUMMER brand that it could hit a home run once more. The emerging HUMMER products signified a change in the timbre of GM's offerings and product development—and in its own confidence in its abilities. "It enabled a great deal of self-confidence," Lutz says. "It told us we could create out of nothing a highly successful premium brand overnight. When we put our minds to it, we can do a vehicle that's better than anything else in its class in the world. Was it GM's mostly clearly defined home run in a long time? Sure. Everybody had to agree, yep they've done it with that."

In particular, the H2 telegraphed to customers that GM was a company once again aiming to build the best products in the world.

As Good As It Gets

As **HUMMER** looks towards the future, it is set to debut its new H2 SUT (Sports Utility Truck) in 2005.

233

"The execution was fabulous," Lutz adds. "It's totally different from the H1 and yet people who are unfamiliar, with it say it looks like an H1."

More important, the H2 and the H1 brought with them a slew of new customers that might not have considered a General Motors product—wealthy, educated customers that are highly coveted within the auto industry. The HUMMER H1, the Humvee-derived model, is said to attract buyers with incomes of more than $200,000 on average, a majority of whom have college degrees and who own five other vehicles. The H2's demographics are somewhat less impressive, but only in comparison with the H1. The H2 also woos buyers with incomes over $200,000, a majority with college degrees—but it's usually the third vehicle in a household.

The HUMMER brand also adds volume to the GM lineup, which is in the final stages of retiring the Oldsmobile brand, which once accounted for more than a million sales a year. HUMMER will come nowhere near those numbers—when all of the new models are available, DiGiovanni predicts the entire line will sell about 100,000 units a year, or about half of what Cadillac sold in 2002—the HUMMERs will contribute to a GM product portfolio much broader than the company had only a decade ago. And, on average, HUMMER shoppers don't leave the dealership without add-ons, about $2000 per customer on average, more than any other GM vehicle.

The HUMMER also serves as a "halo" vehicle, one of the instantly recognizable GM icons, like the Corvette or the Cadillacs, that draws unfamiliar customers into GM showrooms. GM pointedly uses HUMMER in promotions like its "Test Drive" program, where shoppers could drive new GM products and, in some cases, take them home overnight for a more thorough evaluation. The HUMMERs brought new customers into showrooms during Test Drive, GM executives say, and even if they couldn't afford to buy one, many customers left with other GM products instead of ending up behind the wheel of a competitor's car or truck.

And likely most important for GM's Duke-educated CEO Rick Wagoner, HUMMER has done all this heavy lifting and brand-building at a profit. It's been "cheap by any stretch of the imagination," notes engineer Lindensmith. Too, manager DiGiovanni says the brand has exceeded profit targets for 2002 and 2003. Though HUMMER execs won't divulge the magic numbers, some analysts have estimated that GM pockets $18,000 or more on each H2.

Its popularity among non-automotive enthusiasts and shoppers is patently observable. Last Christmas, the radio-controlled HUMMER H2 sold through toy retailers for $99 was one of the most popular toys of the holiday season. And HUMMER gear—everything from work shirts to jackets to mountain bikes to $15 baseball hats—continues to contribute a significant amount of goodwill for the HUMMER brand. The HUMMER name moves more merchandise than any other GM brand, and any of its other vehicles save the Corvette. Even if you can't drive one, it seems, you can own a piece of what has been called the "kick-butt vehicle of all time."

There are signs, however that HUMMER may be peaking in its cultural significance. Already a visible target for the anti-SUV crowd, the H2 begun to attract the kind of trouble that comes with near-universal appeal.

Consider the story of basketball prep star LeBron James. While still in high school, James was investigated for driving a brand-new H2 while contemplating going pro or going to college (eventually deciding to cast his lot in the NBA draft). On the same day that Ohio's High School Athletic Association said his brand-new HUMMER H2 wouldn't disqualify him from playing, an 88-year-old woman filed a police report against James, claiming he'd backed his new $50,000 ride into her car.

The lawsuits directly involving the HUMMER also would kick off fairly early in its lifespan. Sued by Chrysler over a lookalike grille with the Jeep line, GM turned around and sued the tiny Avanti Motor Corporation, based in Villa Rica, Ga., west of Atlanta, over a vehicle dubbed the Studebaker XUV and shown at the 2003 Chicago auto show. The vehicle, sharing the HUMMER H2's proportions but based off of Ford truck components, was to enter production the following year, priced from around $75,000. GM claimed that the Studebaker XUV "knocks off and misappropriates the shape of the world-famous and incredibly popular HUMMER H2 SUV," and sought an injunction against Avanti to keep it from manufacturing, advertising, and selling the XUV. The companies settled the lawsuit, with Avanti agreeing to make design changes to their vehicle—but not before GM appeared petulant for suing the impossibly small carmaker.

With gas prices rising in late 2003, some buyers may have begun to express remorse with the H2's 12-mpg drinking habit. A J.D. Power quality survey for 2003 ranked the H2 at the bottom for initial quality, scoring 225 problems per 100 vehicles in an industry where Lexus was tagged with only 76 problems per car. In the same study other GM brands had shown major improvements, notably Buick's sedans. HUMMER's goal for 2004 is most improved in the Power survey.

The quality issues were followed by more unpleasant tidings in summer 2003, when the company put its first rebate on the H2 since its introduction. At the time holding onto 91 days' worth of vehicles when 60 days is considered normal, the company put the incentives on the vehicle to make way for the 2004 models. Tagged as a way to adjust inventory, the rebates mostly meant that the HUMMER was becoming more like GM's other vehicles, for better or worse.

The road ahead

Americans continue to buy SUVs at record levels, with sales up almost 7 percent last year and up 42 percent over the past five years, according to industry figures. And the HUMMER name continues to carry a luster unavailable to any other SUV brand, even Land Rover—which has the stunning Range Rover to its credit, but an iffy future under the Ford umbrella. But the only thing for sure in HUMMER's future is more models.

This year brings the first major revamp for the H1, the civilian version of the Humvee. Its interior is completely recrafted to give the impression of more interior space and better noise characteristics. New leather seats, suede and leather trim line the cabin, and reshaped central tunnel covers and headliners give more interior storage and at the same time, reduce the visual bulk of the H1's interior. The 6.5-liter turbodiesel V-8 also makes ten more horsepower, for a total of 205 hp, and ten additional pound-feet of torque, for 440 lb-ft in all. A tire inflation system and run-flat tires are now standard in the model that is charged with retaining the HUMMER's brand DNA.

As for the H2, it gains a new model with a pickup bed where the original sports an enclosed cargo area. The H2 SUT is essentially an H2 SUV with a rear bed similar to that in the Chevrolet Avalanche, down to the midgate that flips and folds down to open a 4x6 cargo bed; the key difference in the SUT's midgate is its power-down window, a first for the GM flexibility panel. A new black interior has power front seats with perforated leather, and aluminum touches are applied throughout the cabin. A new navigation system is offered with OnStar and XM Satellite radio. The SUT is expected to account for as many as 15,000 units a year, with some SUV buyers opting for the open truck bed. DiGiovanni says the SUT will give HUMMER the momentum it needs to carry the brand through 2004. "This is going to be a burst of excitement to HUMMER like the H2 was. It's like a convertible hummer. It's like a snub-nosed revolver–it looks like a smaller vehicle," he says.

And in the distance, HUMMER's future lies in smaller, more fuel-efficient vehicles. "We're not anti-fuel efficient or anti-environment," DiGiovanni claims. "Future HUMMERs need to get smaller, need to get fuel-efficient. I'd love to have a fuel-celled H2. Diesels play a role, but it's not the answer. There are negatives to diesels too."

HUMMERs will, in fact be getting smaller–and soon. While Jeep has gone upscale in its intentions, HUMMER is working its way down into new product segments, and will round out its brand in 2006 with an all-new HUMMER H3, derived from GM's new compact pickup truck architecture. "It's going to help us with some people that have a problem with HUMMER because it's more fuel-efficient," DiGiovanni says. The H3 is planned as the volume product in the HUMMER lineup, with a pricetag in the mid-$30,000 range. It will be the first HUMMER built somewhere other than Indiana–its home will be Shreveport, La., where it will be assembled alongside Chevrolet's Colorado and GMC's Canyon trucks.

GM has shown the general direction for the next HUMMER's design, in concept form at the 2004 Los Angeles and Detroit auto shows. Dubbed the H3T, the new HUMMER concept is "a little more environmentally responsible" than what consumers might expect from HUMMER, according to the brand's design director, Clay Dean. The H3T concept, built off the compact truck platform, sported a pickup bed, a flexible interior, an interior design in part with sportswear company Nike, and an unconventional powerplant–a turbocharged in-line five-cylinder engine with 350 hp that could get up to 22 mpg, according to GM's estimates.

By the time the H3 arrives in showrooms, sharing some of the design cues of the H3T concept, the HUMMER brand will also have a new home as a wave of new stand-alone dealerships are opened across the country. Styled like a military-grade Quonset hut with off-road test tracks built into their design, the new showrooms will be opening as the H3 begins to appear in national advertising. "The dealer stores are going to be there when the H3 arrives," DiGiovanni says. "HUMMER stores will be cutting ribbons all over the country. They have to have their store built when H3 arrives sometime in 2005."

The key to the H3, DiGiovanni says, is telegraphing to customers that it is as much a HUMMER as the core H1 and the upmarket H2. "Will it be authentic like a HUMMER off-road and does it look like a HUMMER? There's the same skepticism there," he says.

HUMMER and GM executives, for now, promise that the brand won't be pressured into the kinds of compromises that lead to the spiritual deaths of brands. "We could go more luxurious, but it would have to be in an Abercrombie and Kent kind of way," said Bob Lutz. "On-road performance isn't so much of an issue; zero to sixty...that's not important. But absolute supremacy in the off-road environment is. Regardless of what size HUMMER we make, the killer off-road capability—better than any other commercially available vehicle in the world—must remain."

Lutz adds that HUMMER isn't limited to the SUV body style. As Ford has expanded the notion of what a Lincoln might be with a new four-door pickup, HUMMER too could expand into the truck arena. "A straight pickup could be appealing, an extended-cab pickup off the H2 or H3—for the value of going to the construction site, [driving] the manliest pickup the world has ever seen. We can safely go in the pickup direction," he said.

What HUMMER can't do is go softcore. "The one thing we can't afford to [do] with HUMMER is kinder and gentler," said Lutz. "You'd never do something like the Jeep Liberty, and you'd never do anything like the Jeep Compass concept, where you're basically using the name. Chrysler just announced henceforth that Jeeps will not be held to the standard of crossing the Rubicon. From a volume standpoint, they're doing the right thing probably. You can expand volume—but the image comes down. It's why we won't do a cheaper Cadillac, or a non-super-capable Hummer."

Marketing experts have their doubts about HUMMER's plans to push into smaller, theoretically less profitable segments. HUMMER derives a lot of its brand magic from its exclusivity. And other luxury brands have lost ground by pursuing buyers in the lower reaches of the auto industry. Mercedes-Benz, notably, has trebled its efforts to sell small A-Class vehicles in Europe, and plans to bring an even smaller, Brazilian-built sport-ute to the U.S. in 2006 under its Smart brand. However, Benz also has watched its quality ratings sag as it attempts to service all bandwidths of the market.

The most difficult audiences to please will be the environmentalists and anarchists who attack HUMMERs in print and in deed. As for the brand's plans to move into more fuel-efficient vehicles, the Sierra Club isn't convinced. "GM suggesting that a HUMMER is good for the environment is like suggesting milkshakes help people lose weight," the Club's Brendan Bell told the *New York Times*.

And while HUMMER tries to appeal to customers with lesser means, it may have to defend its very existence should the NHTSA's Corporate Average Fuel Economy (CAFE) rules change. And change is coming, if Dr. Jeffrey Runge's agency fulfills its plan to bring trucks and cars closer together in terms of fuel economy. The agency says it will try to close the loophole that allows trucks to meet significantly less stringent fuel-economy averages than do passenger cars. The NHTSA is studying several ways to evolve the CAFE legislation and right what is by all accounts a legislative failure. When enacted, trucks made up only 20 percent of the U.S. automotive market; now that number has risen to more than 50 percent. Under the Bush administration, the NHTSA already has revised the truck average upward. While cars remain on the hook for a 27.5-mpg fleet average, truck fleets are mandated to average 20.7 mpg for the 2004 model year, with that number rising to 22.2 mpg by the 2007 model year.

The agency is studying a number of ways to bring trucks further to heel. One method would be to set fuel standards for the biggest trucks, including the H2 and H1. The other would dissolve the truck and car distinctions and instead, setting vehicle fuel economy by vehicle weight. Either or both of the proposals could be enacted for the 2008 model year, after a period of public comment. However, problems with both proposals are evident, from how to classify the largest trucks to how to make accommodations for drivers who actually use light-duty trucks for commerce, not for errands.

A modest proposal on modifying our oil-rich taste might involve both of these proposals, plus the kind of "corporate welfare" that's an anathema to both radical liberals and conservatives. A magnitude change in America's oil consumption and in its dependence on energy from foreign sources has to take into account not just automobiles, but megahomes, megamalls, and megaresorts too. But when it comes to automobiles, a game-changing injection of $10 billion or $20 billion—not the paltry $1 billion promised for fuel-cell vehicle research—could pay for the costs for American-based automakers to build American-designed, American-assembled hybrids with 25 to 50 percent better fuel economy than today's vehicles. And it could happen within five years. Detroit rightfully complains that the greens would see them in bankruptcy getting hybrids to market—but given the competitive edge of having their research and development costs underwritten by renewable grants could catapult American automakers to the forefront of the technology while quickly reducing our need for oil from unstable Middle East autocracies. Make the automakers commit to a rigorous schedule: take the cash and increase fuel economy across the entire vehicle fleet, trucks and cars alike, by a minimum of 25 percent, and watch America's true strength emerge. Make it a modern-day space race, a competition–the same kind of competition that resulted in the first Humvee.

While there is no doubt that poorly written legislation played the major role in shifting U.S. buyers to SUVs, a backlash against the SUV backlash will no doubt drive more Americans into the seats of sport-utes. The HUMMER is the ultimate automotive expression of "mind your own business," and protestors like those torching HUMMERs in California aren't weakening SUV lovers' resolve. They're strengthening it. "Do they want us all living in caves, eating grass?" says SUV advocate Vines, now the head of Chrysler Group's public relations team. "SUVs are creating jobs and paying taxes for the country. Automobiles have made our country and have given us a vibrant middle class. Do they have bad side effects? Yes, everything does."

"The SUV jihad over the past few years hasn't really dampened overall demand," says George Peterson, president of consultancy AutoPacific. Petersen's research shows that more than 40 percent of those in the market for a new vehicle are considering a sport-ute for their purchase, a figure higher than for any other type of vehicle. AutoPacific says its research indicates that SUV sales will rise to more than 4 million units by the end of the decade, and the number of individual SUVs on the market will blossom from 50 to more than 80 by 2008.

Those numbers include figures for an emerging market segment known as crossovers. These car-based vehicles have many of the hallmarks of the SUV, including some off-road capability and wagon body styles. But because they're car-based, they tend to be smaller, get better gas mileage while still offering the all-weather capability that most SUV customers seem to need, leaving true off-road capability to the truck-derived utes. The first crossover, AMC's 1980 Eagle, has been succeeded by whole generations of Subaru vehicles, as well as newer entries like the Toyota Highlander, Saturn VUE and the Ford Escape.

Another promising development for the long-term health of the SUV is the arrival of the first hybrid sport-utes. Hybrid vehicles use gas engines teamed with electric motors and batteries to deliver performance equivalent to, or in some cases better than that of purely gas-driven vehicles. Hybrid passengers cars like Toyota's Prius have proven popular with celebrities in a way that couldn't be predicted, often substituting for the ubiquitous SUV as a sort of reverse status symbol for young Hollywood icons like Cameron Diaz and Leonardo diCaprio.

Ford's Escape Hybrid, coming in late 2004, will blend the crossover SUV with the hybrid for a fuel-efficient ute that has wagon versatility with the potential for 40-mpg fuel economy. By teaming a small four-cylinder engine with electric power, Ford hopes to deliver an all-wheel-drive Escape Hybrid with the power of a V-6, 1000 pounds of towing capability and a pricetag competitive with V-6 crossovers while delivering great fuel economy and, as a result, fewer emissions.

The other end of the hybrid SUV market will be charted by Lexus' new RX 400H. While Toyota's less expensive hybrids trumpet their gas-electric powertrains as an economy windfall, the company's upscale brand will use hybrid technology to boost performance without boosting fuel usage or emissions. The RX 400H, an attractively styled crossover SUV, will sport a 3.3-liter V-6 engine teamed with Toyota's Hybrid Synergy Drive system, which it says will deliver the equivalent of 270 horsepower while also delivering fuel economy unheard of in a sport-ute—better than 27.5 mpg, the company says. Priced as the premium product in the RX crossover lineup, the new vehicle will lend a cachet to hybrid power that promises to change the way well-heeled buyers might think about a more fuel-efficient future.

The move to hybrids and crossovers is a natural response to the excesses of the SUV boom. And according to the *New York Times'* Bradsher, it's a welcome move for safety as well. "All of the automakers are working much harder these days to make safer, more fuel-efficient SUVs. When I started writing about crash compatibility in 1997, most automakers made no attempt to measure and reduce the effect of their vehicles on other motorists. The rise of crossover utility vehicles partly reflects an effort to address the safety and environmental problems posed by traditional SUVs. We'll see more crossovers, but body-on-frame architectures will continue to be sold in large numbers."

Instead of swinging from one extreme to the other—barring new federal legislation or CAFE intervention—the SUV of today will continue to mature, encompassing everything from the inexpensive front-drive Honda Element to the $110,000 HUMMER H1. In the words of analyst Daniel Gorrell from consulting firm Strategic Vision, "SUVs are not a fad, nor is this eco-terrorism the beginning of the SUV's downfall."

What's it all about, HUMMER?

HUMMERs are lethal weapons—and toys. They're obnoxiously large vehicles that drink gas or diesel fuel—and do things few other vehicles on the face of the earth can do. They can launch TOW missiles with stunning accuracy, clabber down stone steps like mountain goats, and draw a crowd of teenagers more quickly than a vacant Xbox or Britney Spears.

HUMMER's transition from war wagon to cultural icon owes as much to the history of the SUV as it does to the history of the "American century." Before sport-utility vehicles even existed, the ancestors of HUMMER crawled the earth, evolving their four-wheel-drive systems and adding the wagon bodies necessary to survive and prosper. Many of those ancestors passed away after short, brutal lives, only to pass on their best, most durable DNA.

Born as the result of a sort of high-stakes manufacturing game of craps, HUMMER emerged during peacetime with enough time to prove its versatility and toughness. And when called to active duty, the seminal Humvee performed brilliantly, earning a reputation for lifesaving and etching its seven-slot grille on the American landscape.

An action hero itself, the Humvee caught the eye of that other action hero – the man that would breathe commercial life into the civilian Hummer, making it the ultimate celebrity accessory. And Arnold Schwarzenegger's role in elevating the HUMMER brand into a household icon would only be exceeded by Iraq's Saddam Hussein, who in two conflicts with the U.S. granted it virtually exclusive airtime for weeks at a time, showing off its most admirable traits, casting it as the steroidally developed wartime hero.

It would be up to General Motors to take over where AM General could not—to take the HUMMER brand from the small time to the very big time. With its vast resources, GM was able to quickly develop and conceive of a whole lineup of HUMMERs capitalizing on the original's essence, while making them more suitable for today's SUV reality. As Harley-Davidson had steered its brand into utter merchandising dominance, GM took little HUMMER and transformed it into the planet's most capable sport-utility vehicle for civilians, bar none.

As soon as GM brought the HUMMER to fruition, circumstances shifted from favorable to fraught with peril—and still HUMMER thrived. Wars with Afghanistan, Iraq and lesser-known terrors engulfed a whole presidential administration, and terrorists at home turned their environmental fury against the new scourge—but HUMMER prospered. Even the capture of Hussein and the election of Schwarzenegger to California's governorship seemed less than coincidental, linking global and national politics once more to HUMMER's present and future.

Competition is perpetual in the auto industry, and HUMMER won't have its militaristic image and testosterone-fueled persona to itself forever. Revived versions of the Ford Bronco and Toyota Land Cruiser are coming with retro style and military overtones, as is a full-size Jeep. But none of those save Jeep will have the overt military connection of the HUMMER, nor its reputation for drawing enemy fire from Iraqis and Arianna Huffington alike.

HUMMER will live long beyond the SUV as a symbol of a Pax Americana, an age in which a hallmark of American strength and ingenuity has cowed its enemies in combat and on the highway. It's joined the nation's pop iconography, and for now, that symbolism is as good as it gets. If GM retreats from the off-road capability or smaller power, HUMMERs will no longer authentic. If AM General doesn't succeed in years to come up with a replacement, that crucial DNA will have been consigned to history. The most frightening future for every American would be Humvees used by terrorists in a homeland attack. HUMMER's image would be shattered, as easily as $5 a gallon gas would ruin the marketing position of an increasingly mainstream brand.

Whether for good or for now, this tiny truck company has become a very big deal, thanks in part to an unrepentant Saddam Hussein, an enthusiastic Arnold Schwarzenegger, and the shrewd execs now running General Motors. Because of them, HUMMER's not going anywhere any time soon—unless it's to Tehran, Pyongyang, or an air-conditioned four-car garage in Brentwood.

Resources

Interviews

Craig Mac Nab, AM General
Michael DiGiovanni, HUMMER
Marc Hernandez, HUMMER
Ken Lindensmith, HUMMER
Keith Bradsher, *New York Times*
Dale Sizemore

Books

Bradsher, Keith. *High and Mighty: SUVS: The World's Most Dangerous Vehicles and How They Got That Way*. New York, NY. PublicAffairs/Perseus Books, 2002.

Lamm, John and Matt DeLorenzo. *Hummer H2*. Osceola, WI. Motorbooks International, 2002.

Munro, Bill. *Humvee*. Wiltshire, UK. The Crowood Press Ltd., 2002

Newspapers

Banerjee, Neela (2003). Pushing Energy Conservation Into the Back Seat of the S.U.V. *New York Times,* 22 November.

Vartabedian, Ralph (2003). Speaking Out On The Perils of SUVs. *The Los Angeles Times.* 22 January.

Kiley, David (2003). Persian Gulf star Humvee back in spotlight. *USA TODAY,* 23 March.

Burns, John F. (2003). A Small Piece of Fiber on Ground Yields Big Payoff for U.S. *New York Times,* 15 December.

DeBarros, Anthony (2003). New baby boom swamps colleges. *USA TODAY,* 1 January.

Pine, Art (2003). U.S. Soldiers Killed, 24 Hurt During U.N. Sweep in Somalia. *Los Angeles Times,* 5 October.

Magazines

Segal, Troy (1991). From Desert Storm, An Urban Dune Buggy? *Business Week,* 18 March. 133.

Shnayerson, Michael (2003). Devastating Luxury: Five years

after Ira Rennert broke ground in a Hamptons potato field for what is now the largest residential compound in America....*Vanity Fair,* July. 128.

Patton, Phil (2002). Car Shrinks. *Fortune Advisor,* 18 March. 187.

Wattenberg, Daniel (1994). Humvee! *Forbes FYI,* 8 November. 116

Electronic Documents

BBC (2000). Flashback: Invasion of Kuwait. 1 August. http://news.bbc.co.uk/2/hi/world/middle_east/856009.stm

Van Dyke, Geoff (2001). Battling "CNN Syndrome." *Folio,* 1 October. http://foliomag.com/ar/battling_cnn_syndrome/

McIntyre, Jamie (2000). Clinton wants biggest boost in defense spending since Reagan. 24 January.
http://www.cnn.com/2000/ALLPOLITICS/stories/01/24/pentagon.budget/

Bartlett, Bruce (1998). Defense Spending Cuts Helped Balance Budget. 9 February. National Center for Policy Analysis; http://www.ncpa.org/oped/bartlett/feb998.html

Center for Defense Information (1994). AMERICA'S DEFENSE MONITOR. 1 November.
http://www.cdi.org/adm/Transcripts/802/

North Atlantic Treaty Organization (1999). NATO's role in relation to the conflict in Kosovo. 15 July.
http://www.nato.int/kosovo/history.htm

Cable News Network. The Museum of Broadcast Communications.
http://www.museum.tv/archives/etv/C/htmlC/cable-newsne/cablenewsne.htm

Sisk, Richard (2003). Iraq toll tops '91: Total now 294 after two U.S. soldiers killed. *New York Daily News,* 13 September.
http://www.nydailynews.com/front/story/117234p-105701c.html

Goodale, Natalie (2003). Lack of armor? *CNC Sunday,* 7 December.
http://www.metrowestdailynews.com

ScienceDaily.com (2002). U.S. Navy Answers Olympian Call, 11 February.
http://www.sciencedaily.com/releases/2002/02/020211080250.htm

Competitive Enterprise Institute
www.cei.org

National Highway Traffic Safety Administration–Corporate Average Fuel Economy (CAFE) rules
http://www.nhtsa.dot.gov/cars/rules/cafe/index.htm

TheCarConnection.com

TheCarConnection.com (2001). Firestone Recalls Millions of Tires. 14 January.
http://www.thecarconnection.com/index.asp?article=3192

Eisenstein, Paul A. (2000). Ford Says Its SUVs Will Get "Green." 28 July.
http://www.thecarconnection.com/index.asp?article=1120

Szczesny, Joseph (2003). SUV Slam: NHTSA Boss Blasts Utes. 20 January.
http://www.thecarconnection.com/index.asp?article=5688

Szczesny, Joseph (2003). Welburn to Head GM Design. 29 September.
http://www.thecarconnection.com/index.asp?article=6473

Eisenstein, Paul A. (2001). Zarrella To Leave GM for B&L, 19 November.
http://www.thecarconnection.com/index.asp?article=4386

Photo Credits

Photos courtesy of AM General:
Pages 33, 40, 42, 48, 56, 59, 65, 73, 81, 99, 105, 115, 133, 201, 207, 214

Photos courtesy of General Motors:
17, 24, 85, 88, 96, 119, 124, 141, 149, 153, 157, 164, 169, 173, 179, 183, 192, 199, 223, 227, 233

Index

Afghanistan, 107, 200, 201, 206, 208, 225
Aidid, Mohammed Farah, 104
AM General, 10, 12–14, 16, 24, 38, 44, 49, 50, 52–55, 57–64, 66–69, 71, 80, 82, 86, 90–92, 94, 95, 101–103, 107, 114, 117, 118, 123, 126, 135–138, 142, 145, 147, 148, 150, 153–156, 159, 161–163, 171, 175, 176, 203, 210
AMC
    Concord, 27
    Eagle, 26, 27, 243
American Motors Corp. (AMC), 11, 26–28, 35, 49, 58
American Petroleum Institute, 114
Anti-SUV, 181, 182, 184, 187, 193–195, 200, 203
Armour, Arnold, 129, 150, 163
Armour, Jim, 50, 91, 103, 118, 132, 134, 135, 147
Army Rangers, 104, 106
Becker, Daniel, 114, 198
Besserdich, William, 22
Black Hawk Down, 104, 117
Blitzer, Wolf, 78
Boone, Pat, 213
Bowden, Mark, 106
Bradsher, Keith, 189, 190

Bryan, Bill, 32
Bush, George H.W., 74, 77, 79, 80, 99, 194, 196
Bush, George W., 13, 112, 177, 202, 203, 205, 206, 210, 216
Butler, George, 93
Cadillac
    Eldorado, 25
    Escalade, 172, 174
CAFE (Corporate Average Fuel Economy), 28–32, 36, 38
Carlsson, Erik, 93
Carter, Jimmy, 69, 108
Cherry, Wayne, 126–129, 135, 145, 146, 150, 155
Chevrolet
    Avalanche, 130
    Bel Air, 25
    Blazer, 32, 38, 122, 231
    Cavalier, 139
    El Camino, 20
    Suburban, 19, 32, 180
    Tahoe, 139, 148, 151, 172
Clancy, Tom, 12, 94
Clinton, William Jefferson, 80, 99–101, 103, 108, 112–114, 118, 176
CNN, 70, 75, 78, 82, 107, 110, 204
Cold War, 90, 101

HUMMER

DaimlerChrysler, 34, 49, 50, 52, 129, 142, 176
    Land Cruiser, 131
    PT Cruiser, 21, 120
Davis, Gray, 218, 224, 227
Davis, Michael, 23
Dean, Clay, 140, 146, 148, 158, 238
DeLorean, John, 134
DeLorenzo, Matt, 91, 132
Delvalle, Eric, 70
Department of Defense, 58
Department of Transportation (DOT), 20
Desert Storm, 131, 171
DiGiovanni, Mike, 129, 130, 132, 134, 135, 139, 140, 142, 145, 163, 165, 166, 167, 204, 205, 235, 237–239
Dodge
    Ram, 123
    Ramcharger, 32
Duvalier, Jean-Claude, 107, 108
Eaton, Bob, 121
Edgar, Bob, 194
Estrada, Erik, 93
Estrala, Angel, 77
Ford
    Bronco, 19, 32, 34, 38, 246
    Escape, 159, 243
    Explorer, 21, 34, 35, 59, 117, 122, 185
    Land Rover, 32, 87, 123, 159, 217
    Range Rover, 32, 34 122, 217, 236
Ford Jr., Clay, 194
Ford Motor Company, 30, 34, 50
Foreman, George, 94
Franken, Al, 187
Franks, Tommy, 206
Frey, Donald, 34
General Motors, 11, 13, 14, 16, 19, 26, 30, 35, 50, 55, 92, 120–123, 125–127, 129–131, 136, 137, 140, 142, 143, 145, 146, 148, 151–156, 161, 166, 167, 171, 175, 181, 188, 236, 246
Detroit Project, 188, 198
Giuliani, Rudy, 175
Gore, Al, 10, 112, 113, 206
Great Depression, 46, 101
Gulf War, 11, 76–78, 80, 112
H1, 11, 15, 16, 147, 149, 166, 171, 172, 199, 202, 204, 207, 216, 223, 232, 234, 237, 241
H2, 11, 13–16, 24, 129, 133, 147, 148, 150–152, 155, 156, 158–163, 166, 168, 170–176, 180, 182, 188, 192, 202, 211–213, 215, 225, 232, 234–239, 241
H3, 238, 239
Hackworth, David, 108
Haiti, 107–110, 117
Hall, Rod, 160
Hernandez, Marc, 142–144, 203
Honda, 28, 210
    Element, 21, 244
Huffington, Arianna, 187
Humvee, 55, 56, 58, 60–62, 66, 67, 70–73, 82, 83, 86, 87, 91, 95, 103–107, 109–112, 118, 127, 128, 139, 145, 148, 161, 163, 171, 172, 174, 177, 202, 209–212, 230–232, 237, 241
Hussein, Qusay, 72
Hussein, Saddam, 11, 13, 71, 72, 75, 78–80, 82, 85, 112, 113, 116, 189, 208, 229, 230, 245, 246
Hussein, Uday, 72
Insurance Institute for Highway Safety, 195
Iraq, 71, 72, 74, 79, 80, 93, 95, 113, 200, 201, 204, 209, 210, 229
James, LeBron, 235
Jameson, Jenna, 94
Jeep, 13, 22, 23, 34, 47, 50, 76, 123, 143, 159, 176, 232, 236, 239
    Cherokee, 26, 27
    Grand Cherokee, 21, 35, 117, 128
    Liberty, 27, 239
    Station Wagon, 23
    Wagoneer, 25–27
    Wrangler, 131
John North Willys, 46
Jones, James Earl, 93
Kaiser, Henry J., 47
Kaiser-Jeep Corporation, 25, 47
Kazman, Sam, 198
King, Don, 95
Kosovo, 111, 112, 117
Kuwait, 71, 72, 74, 75, 77–80, 82, 112, 113, 159
Laden, Osama Bin, 206, 208, 229
Lamm, John, 132
Leff, Roger, 110
Lindensmith, Ken, 155, 156, 160, 162, 234
Lutz, Robert A., 150, 153, 154, 183, 232, 239
Mac Nab, Craig, 60, 62–64, 66–72, 82, 92, 103, 201, 210, 231

Index

Major, John, 75
Mauldin, Bill, 23
McCain, John, 100
McManus, Walter, 37
Nader, Ralph, 181
Nasser, Jac, 121, 123, 186, 195
National Center of Policy Analysis (NCPA), 100
National Highway Traffic Safety Administration (NHTSA), 20, 29, 30, 32, 181, 185, 196, 197, 240
Noriega, Manuel, 69–71, 74, 76
North American International Auto Show, 128, 150
North Atlantic Treaty Organization (NATO), 112
Operation Desert Shield, 72, 75
Operation Desert Storm, 71, 75, 77, 101, 103, 117, 127, 208, 231
Operation Iraqi Freedom, 145, 210
Operation Joint Guardian, 112
Operation Restore Hope, 107
Panama, 70, 71
Patton, Phil, 39
Perot, H. Ross, 99
Pontiac Aztek, 132
Rapaille, Clothaire, 39
Reagan, Ronald, 37, 58, 78, 218, 228
Rennert, Ira, 102, 103
Richardson, William R., 78
Rockwell, Norman, 98
Runge, Jeffrey, 28, 196
Safety, 185, 196, 197
Saturn VUE, 243
Schwarzenegger, Arnold, 11–13, 83, 85–87, 89–94, 98, 133, 162, 165, 166, 174, 175, 203, 217–222, 224, 227, 228, 245, 246
Serbia, 111
Shahan, Rosemary, 197
Shriver, Maria, 92, 163
Sierra Club, 114, 116, 117, 176, 181, 198, 213, 215, 240
Sizemore, Dale, 104
Smith, Jack, 119
Smith, Roger, 122
Somalia, 103, 104, 106, 107, 110, 117
Souter, David, 196
Special Ops military, 43, 44
Sport utility vehicle (SUV), 19–22, 25, 26, 30, 32, 34–36, 38, 39, 41, 42, 45, 116, 117, 120, 122, 123, 125, 131, 139, 148, 153, 159, 167, 170, 175, 176, 180, 181, 184, 185, 187–191, 193, 197, 203, 215, 243–245
Sport-utility trucks (SUT), 20
Steele, Mike, 104
Stern, Howard, 93
Sudan, 107
Sunday, Brian, 109
Taguiri, John, 180, 186
Taliban, 206, 208
Ternes, Pete, 213
Thieme, Mark, 77
Toyota, 28, 120
   Highlander, 243
   Land Cruiser, 19, 32, 246
Turner, Ted, 94
Tyson, Mike, 94
U.S. Army, 60, 62, 66, 68–70, 76, 104, 109, 118, 230
U.S. Border Patrol, 33
U.S. Marines, 70, 77
U.S. military, 11–13, 15, 24, 44, 45, 47, 63, 76, 80, 90, 95, 98, 100, 177, 182, 202, 230
United Nations (U.N.), 78, 79, 113
United Nations Security Council, 75, 108
V-6 engine, 243
V-8 engine, 30, 52, 97, 148, 150, 237
Vietnam War, 50, 58, 62, 78, 82, 100
Vines, Jason, 194
Volkswagen (VW), 28
Volkswagen Beetle, 28
Wagoner, Rick, 122, 125, 154, 235
Wahlberg, Mark, 117
Weber, Bill, 76
Williams, Montel, 94
Willys-Overland Motors, Inc., 46, 47
Wilson, Pete, 218
World War I, 22, 74
World War II, 23, 26, 45, 75, 230, 232
Zachow, Otto, 22
Zarrella, Ron, 132, 134, 151, 152, 165

Other Motorbooks International titles of interest include

Hummer: The Next Generation
ISBN 0-7603-0045-3

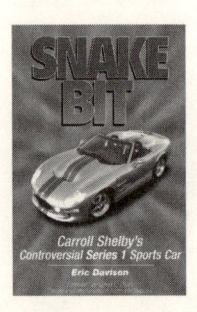

Snake Bit
ISBN 0-7603-1781-X

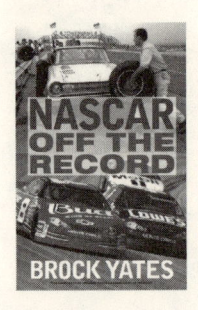

NASCAR Off the Record
ISBN 0-7603-1726-7

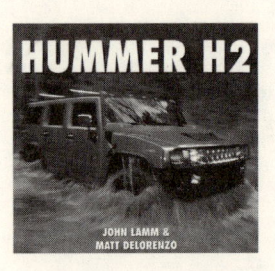

Hummer H2
ISBN 0-7603-1244-3

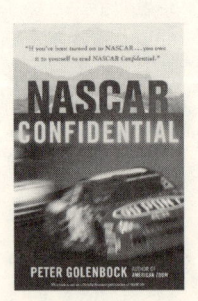

NASCAR Confidential
ISBN 0-7603-1483-7

4-Wheeler's Bible
ISBN 0-7603-1056-4